Contrary to popular belief, Christians do not need another book on sexuality. We have enough rules, enough diatribes, enough proclamations, enough condemning screeds. Thankfully, *My Exodus* is not another book composed by Alan. Alan doesn't address the messiness of sexuality matters. He reminds us that God loves everyone equally regardless of their sexual orientation or practices. In a time when so many people are searching for easy answers, Chambers teaches us to wrestle with difficult questions and empowers us to search for truth with grace. *My Exodus* is part memoir and part guidebook, but wholeheartedly hopeful. If you're struggling with how to live well or love well, you can't afford not to read this book.

— **Jonathan Merritt**, author, *Jesus Is Better Than You Imagined*; senior columnist, Religion News Service

In an atmosphere of anger, hatred, and division, Alan Chambers is a voice of love, authenticity, sanity, and truth. *My Exodus* is a book that should be read by all who want to know a better way. Alan Chambers "smells like Jesus."

— **Steve Brown**, seminary professor, broadcaster, author, and founder of Key Life Network

Alan Chambers' well-publicized exodus from Exodus International has a backstory that needs to be heard. People on all sides of the LGBTQ issue will benefit from seeing the story's protagonists humanized rather than stigmatized, and this account, beautifully told, does so with grace and honesty.

— **Brian D. McLaren**, author/activist, *brianmclaren.net*

Exodus International promised to change gay to straight, but instead found itself changed from a large, influential organization to one with shuttered doors. President Alan Chambers advocated orientation change in both his personal and professional lives, and instead found himself changed as a man and as a leader: keeping his vows to his wife and children, directing courageous organizational change, and experiencing and proclaiming Jesus' love. At first glance, *My Exodus* seems like a story of deep and often painful change, but read it more closely, or read it a second time, and you'll see that the really true things have stayed the same. God's changeless love and boundless grace were the true promise, not orientation change. Alan describes how truth, grace, love, and mercy have proven solid and trust-worthy, even through profound organizational and personal challenges. The time is ripe—overripe—for truth-telling about reparative therapy and about the sincere spiritual lives of gay Christians. This book tells that truth.

—Jenell Paris, professor of anthropology, Messiah College; author, *The End of Sexual Identity*

Who is spotless in this world except the Lamb of God? Who extends the unmerited favor of grace to all mankind but the Lord? Read this honest, open, personal, and loving work and see how the God of love meets us at every point of our need and restores us by his grace as we walk through the temptations and potholes of life.

—Rev. Dr. Thelma Wells, CEO, That a Girl and Friends Speakers Agency and Enrichment Tours

My Exodus is one of those rare books that I could not put down until I finished it. While it will certainly be controversial, I promise it is not dull! Alan and Leslie share their journey with amazing vulnerability and honesty. Five stars!

— Clark Whitten, pastor, Grace Church; author, *Pure Grace*

My Exodus is beautifully written. You will laugh and cry, but most of all you will encounter an extraordinary grace. Thank you, Alan and Leslie, for allowing us into those vulnerable places.

— Debra Hirsch, author, *Untamed* and *Redeeming Sex*

The Bible says that the truth that you know will set you free, and this is what happened for Alan Chambers when he was challenged by a young gay man in the Exodus International ministry who knew that heterosexual marriage would never be a solution for his life. *My Exodus* is a story of courage, truth, and integrity as Alan Chambers, the final president of Exodus International, closes the doors of the organization, along with its premise of change, and embarks on a whole new adventure with his wife, Leslie, of love, grace, acceptance, and inclusion.

— Rev. Sandra Turnbull, pastor, The Glory Center; author, *God's Gay Agenda*

You don't know what you think you know about an issue until you know someone deeply affected by the issue. This book, written by two people I deeply respect, is not only delightful and intriguing but profoundly insightful.

— Dr. Joel C. Hunter, senior pastor, Northland — A Church Distributed, Orlando

Grateful for the honesty and bravery that Alan and Leslie willingly share in their story. I'm hopeful their book sheds light and brings hope to many who are confused and hurting, especially in the Christian community. Like the Chambers, I've also found new freedom in loving everyone and seeing the image of God in all of humanity.

—Kim Hill, Grammy-nominated, Dove-Award-winning recording artist

Alan and Leslie have written a quick read with high value. If you're curious about the closing of Exodus International, because of Alan's vulnerability you'll learn how the decision was made. Decide for yourself whether it is something to blame him for or credit him with. But this book is about so much more. Your hope and confidence will increase if you're willing to think about some of Alan's statements that may surprise and even challenge you. Alan's most important contribution might be in the area of identity. *My Exodus* is a powerful reminder that knowing who we really are is transforming and energizing. Authenticity is a beautiful thing, and Alan's example might just move you to examine your own life. You will benefit from Alan's humbling and vulnerable slice-of-life illustrations. Read this book now.

—Kathy Koch, president and founder, Celebrate Kids, Inc., *www.DrKathyKoch.com*

MY EXODUS

FROM FEAR TO GRACE

ALAN CHAMBERS

WITH LESLIE CHAMBERS

ZONDERVAN

My Exodus

Copyright © 2015 by Alan Chambers and Leslie Chambers

This title is also available as a Zondervan ebook. Visit www.zondervan.com/ebooks.

Requests for information should be addressed to:
Zondervan, 3900 Sparks Dr. SE, Grand Rapids, Michigan 49546

Library of Congress Cataloging-in-Publication Data

Chambers, Alan, 1972–
    My exodus : from fear to grace / Alan Chambers, with Leslie Chambers.
      pages cm
    ISBN 978-0-310-34248-9 (softcover)
     1. Chambers, Alan, 1972– 2. Chambers, Leslie. 3. Church work with gays.
    4. Homosexuality—Religious aspects—Christianity. I. Chambers, Leslie. II. Title.
    BR1702.C43 2015
    277.3'083092—dc23   [B] 2015022449

Published in association with the literary agency of Legacy, LLC, Winter Park, FL 32789

Cover design: James Hall
Cover photography: Edward Linsmier
Interior design: Kait Lamphere

First printing July 2015 / Printed in the United States of America

For Isaac and Molly

CONTENTS

FOREWORD

Ten years ago, if someone told me that Alan Chambers would ask me to write the foreword for his book, I likely would have reacted with utter disbelief. In fact, the decision to actually agree was not one that was arrived at easily. I haven't exactly been shy about the fact that I have been a staunch defender of gay people all of my life. I've always believed that people are born gay and should be able to live freely without question or condemnation. As such, Alan Chambers is a very controversial man.

My first encounter with Alan Chambers came in the summer of 2010 during the Exodus International annual conference, when I was an executive producer and host of *Our America* on the Oprah Winfrey Network (OWN). Since its inception, Exodus International, of which Alan was president, preached "change is possible," that people who were gay could, through prayer, self-help efforts, or reparative therapy, become straight. To the surprise of my colleagues and me, Exodus agreed to allow our cameras into the conference for an unprecedented look inside. The caveat was that, to protect people's privacy, we would not be able to shoot any of the workshops, and we had to set up our cameras in the back of the room and not shoot anyone's face.

I remember vividly the enormous, dark auditorium and the thousands of people who filled it. It was clear that I was in a massive space with people who didn't want others to know they were there. Acknowledging their presence meant that they might have "same sex attraction," something people there wanted desperately to try to change about themselves. I recall seeing a young boy who looked to be around fifteen years old, and the scene made me sad. I wanted to grab the boy, hug him, and tell him that God loved him, exactly how he was, and that nobody should try to make him change.

While at the conference, I was also granted an interview with Alan. I'd seen him on television before and I was always struck by how poised and unflappable he was. I also, incidentally, couldn't help noticing how gay he seemed. Given my hard-and-fast beliefs about homosexuality, I was, admittedly and distastefully, eager to observe Alan living a lie, a lie that I'd assumed was meant to suggest that because Alan was happily married to a woman, others who were struggling with "same sex attraction" could do the same, that they could change.

In the end, however, it is Alan who has changed. Not from gay to straight, not from "conservative" to "liberal," but instead, from condemning to accepting, from being ashamed to being freed. And I am certain that his journey, and that of his wife, Leslie, can help people similarly come to terms with and love the person they are, regardless of what others think of them. By his own admission, by trying to help people achieve something impossible, Alan, as head of Exodus, had hurt some people. Now he cares more that others believe that God loves them, irrespective of their sexual orientation or anything else, for that matter.

Alan writes about our first interaction during the conference further on in this book, but I would actually go on to spend more time with him and his lovely wife in later years—at their home with their children, on a television set, at their church, and on the phone. What I would come to believe is that Alan *is* happily married to Leslie, but that they do not want their relationship to be an example of how a homosexual man can live in heterosexual bliss. They no longer want to be heralded as a gay-to-straight success story. Rather, theirs is a relationship that *all* couples, straight, gay, or whatever, can derive inspiration from. This is the story of their sojourn to grace, of their big "come to Jesus" moment.

I long for a time when we will cease to feel the need to characterize and criticize other people, a time when we will just love. After reading this sometimes uncomfortably honest and brave book, it's clear that Alan and Leslie want that also.

—*Lisa Ling, www.LisaLing.com*

PREFACE

Alan and I were recently asked, "Why write a book?" It's a good question, and my initial response was, "I don't know." How's that for inspiring? Our life together, in many ways, is so completely commonplace I imagined our book would be drudgery to read. Of course, thinking for a moment longer, I get that there is a thread of the extraordinary spun into the fabric of our ordinary lives.

This book is simply our story. It's a story about our parents, our childhood, our coming of age, our marriage, and our journey out of a system of beliefs driven by fear and rules and shame, a system steeped in a condemning mindset toward gay people. This is a story about life within the confines of God's love and grace. It's about relationships, and it has a happy ending.

Our pastor of twenty years, Clark Whitten, once shared a picture with our church that portrays a marked fabric. It's a picture of a woman who is caught in the throes of adultery in a society where such actions call for her to be put to death. The community's religious leaders brought her before a man who claimed to know God. The man, Jesus, had grown up in the very religious system the men led, and taught from the same religious literature they stood upon, yet to those leaders, he propagated heresy. Instead of rendering God as a distant, angry judge who demanded perfect obedience to set rules, this Jesus taught about God as a loving, intimate father. He spoke of not condemning people. He spoke of love, a love that is available to everyone. It was a radical love that resonated with ordinary people and had an extraordinary effect.

Oh, how the religious leaders thought they had Jesus backed into a religious corner. If he had shown this sinful woman the kind of love he claimed to offer, he would mock their laws. If he condemned her as was required by their laws, his ministry would be impotent. Of course, Jesus chose not to answer their accusations. He didn't condone her behavior. He didn't condemn her behavior. He simply wrote something in the sand and stated that if they were going to fulfill the law and stone her to death, then the man who had no sin should throw the first stone. One by one, each man laid down his stone and walked away.

Many in the Christian church know this story and have been taught that we shouldn't condemn. Great. It's a good lesson, but we've missed another life-giving truth this story offers. When the men chose not to condemn — because they were unable to when faced with their own humanity — they walked away and left the woman alone with Jesus. And there is no better place to find oneself than alone with Jesus. And Jesus, everything he said and everything he did, points to a loving, gracious Father God.

Alan and I have found ourselves alone with Jesus, and it's extraordinary, and that's why we wrote this book.

—*Leslie Chambers*

ACKNOWLEDGMENTS

Leslie and I treasure people, especially our people—the ones with whom we live our daily lives. Without each of you, this book would not be. You all enrich our lives.

First, Isaac and Molly, thank you both for letting us spend so much time on this book. We love you both with our whole hearts and are so proud of the people you are. You make us laugh, and every day is better with both of you in it.

We owe so much to our family. Our moms, Betty Chambers and Susan Paull, who encourage us, fight for us, and serve as two of our biggest cheerleaders. To both of our dads, Bob Chambers and Bob Paull, whose dear voices we regularly hear encouraging us from heaven.

Between us, Leslie and I have seven amazing siblings, seven wonderful siblings-in-law, thirty-five nieces and nephews, and eighteen great nieces and nephews and counting. Everyone should have such a family. We love each of you dearly.

Grace Church—Clark and Martha, you ruined us with grace and we are so grateful. Grace Church staff, elders, worship team, congregation, and youth—it is with all of you we not only are learning about the goodness of God but are practically living out a life in which his grace changes everything. You are our brothers and sisters, and again, everyone should have such a family.

To the families Chase, Salisbury, and Hernandez: thank you for doing *real* life with us. Al, Kim, and Niquette kids, Randy Thomas, and Gloria Warden—our throats close and our eyes fill with tears; few words could do our friendships justice. We love you all.

DJ Snell, our dear, dear friend who introduced us and happens to be our agent and fellow architect of so many important structures we've built together, life is far better with you in it. As it is with Barb, Angela, Neal, Jamie, Quinton, Jordan, Orel, Tiffany, and Bobby.

To many of those once connected with Exodus who walked with us—board, staff, leaders, men, women, couples, parents, youth, and givers. To Dr. Kathy Koch, whose friendship is invaluable. To Scott Dolbear, who stuck with us to the end.

To those who were hurt by me or people and systems within Exodus: may you experience peace, healing, and rest believing in and receiving God's perfect and abundant love.

Thank you Fresno and Winter Park/Orlando friends who held on to us when our dads passed away. And ICS for being such a vital community for us and our kids.

Thank you, David Morris, Tom Dean, and Zondervan, for believing in us and taking on this project.

Carolyn McCready—there wouldn't be a book without you. Nicci Jordan Hubert—best editor ever. You both are life changers and we consider ourselves amazingly (sorry to use this word, 'cause it sounds so cheesy, but we really mean it) blessed to have worked with you. You are beautiful and smart and funny and real and really good at what you do.

To *Mine* from *Yours*: ILYSM.

INTRODUCTION

"What's up, Matt?" I said, trying to mute my exasperation. "You okay?"

My employee, Matt, had been moping around the Exodus International office for a week. I'd noticed a pretty dramatic dip in his productivity too, and several people on our team had been walking on eggshells around him, wondering whether we'd done something to offend him. So I had called him into my office that summer morning in 2006 to give him the opportunity to open up, but his blank stare and subsequent downward gaze signaled to me that he wasn't about to jump at the opportunity to spill his guts. What followed were a few minutes of very uncomfortable silence—Matt, face toward the floor, fidgeting with the zipper on his hoodie, and me, somehow increasingly mesmerized by the ingenuity of zippers in general.

I'm an extrovert and an outward processor. I don't care much for awkward silence and staring contests. But I was determined to let this one go on past my normal point of discomfort. Something serious was going on with Matt, and it was important for me to hear him. Over the past few days, my mind had tried to fill in the blanks as to why he had been so closed off.

Could Matt be struggling with same-sex attraction more than normal? Was he on the brink of giving up? Has he done something wrong? What could be so awful that he would walk out of a staff meeting five minutes into it and not return for more than an hour? I carried on this inner dialogue while staring at Matt's fidgeting hands, and my impatience percolated. Personal struggles were no excuse for professional irresponsibility. As the silence ticked on, my swivel chair rotated right and my gaze drifted past my office wall of framed photos—a shot of Leslie and our two adopted kids, Isaac and Molly, both one year old at the time; one of Leslie and me with Governor Jeb Bush; one of Mike Huckabee and me talking at an event; a commemoration of one of my many visits to the White House, which in this instance had been a small gathering with President Bush announcing his support for the Federal Marriage Amendment—and moved toward the window, which showcased a collection of maple trees swaying in the summer breeze. In typical Orlando fashion, it was humid outside, but from my air-conditioned office, the sun and the warmth from the window felt downright cheery. Too cheery for the moment.

And then, Matt finally spoke. "I'm never going to be like you."

I was shocked. I swiveled my chair back to center and leaned my arms on my desk. "What do you mean?" I felt a sense of dread. I knew where this was going.

"I'm never going to be *straight* like you. I'll never have a wife and kids like you. I'll never be healed like you." Matt's words were slow and calm. "Alan, how can I be like you?"

I'd been asked the question a thousand times before throughout my long career at Exodus International, and especially during my presidency. But it had always been indirect, couched in acceptable Christian terms, such as, "Is healing or freedom from homosexuality possible?" Anyone looking at me, a happily married, "formerly" gay man with two kids and a dog, listening to what I had to say, knowing anything about the organization I led, would assume my answer would be an unequivocal yes. And they were always right: I always said yes. But this time was different. Something about Matt's vulnerability and the simplicity of his message—and something about the condition of my heart in that moment—allowed his words to drive in.

Even if I'd wanted to, I couldn't have summoned the energy or the will to become defensive or to spout the same old rhetoric that had become so familiar to me. Instead, Matt's admission opened a floodgate of questions about my own realities. *What have I done?* I thought. *Am I a fraud? Why does he think I'm the goal? I've hurt this kid. Are there others? Oh, dear God. There are others. I have to be honest. But this conversation might change everything.* The chaos of my internal chatter was like the static of truckers talking over a crowded CB radio.

Here I was, the thirty-four-year-old leader of the

ex-gay world. I was in my fifth year as president of Exodus International. At that point, Exodus was a thirty-year-old global umbrella organization for a large and fast-growing network of Christian ministries, counselors, and churches seeking to help those struggling with unwanted same-sex attractions. It was a world where thousands of people wrestled with and sought to reconcile their faith and sexuality. It was a world where homosexuality was considered a sin, displeasing to God, and something to overcome.

Exodus was also a fundamental part of my own story. On that day, with a wife of eight years and two gorgeous children, I was the quintessential picture of an Exodus success. Our story had become *the* story many leaders in the evangelical church told when the question of whether someone could change from gay to straight was asked. It was my story, and I shared it every opportunity I had.

But Matt's statement somehow uncovered in me an aspect of my story I didn't tell as often, at least not publicly. I loved my life, my story, and my job of proclaiming that freedom from homosexuality is possible. But the truth that hit me in that moment created a fissure in the foundation of the story I'd been telling for years.

I knew in that moment that something had shifted, but what I didn't realize was that my entire life was about to dramatically change.

Matt was a kindhearted and side-splittingly funny blond pastor's kid from a small town in Central California.

I met him in 2000 after I taught a workshop on homosexuality at a mega, bicoastal Christian event for youth called DC/LA. Fresh out of high school, he was the first kid to get to me after the session was over. He was with a group of kids from his church and he readily shared that "this"—the generic and safe-feeling term so many people used to describe their attraction to the same gender—was a large part of his story. Like everyone I've ever met in the Church with "this struggle," Matt was beyond ready to connect with others who could relate. Like WWII vets who meet by chance and become instant brothers, Matt enlisted in the ex-gay army that day and became an immediate comrade and friend.

Through email and AOL instant messages, the only popular versions of social media at the time, I stayed in touch with Matt and we became friends. Leslie had grown up near Matt's home, so every time we visited her family, we spent time with him too.

A couple of years later, after I became the president of Exodus International, I started growing the budget and adding staff. I reached out to Matt. He was a budding writer, leading young adult groups for the local Exodus ministry in his area, and was interested in working for Exodus and for me. Long story short, I hired him to work in the Exodus Youth department and he moved crosscountry to Orlando.

Matt was a delight. He channeled his gifts for writing, humor, and graphic design into his work at Exodus, but like many others before and after him, the ministry eventually began to sap some of his joy, creativity, and hope. He was lethargic, not getting his work done. Reclusive. Not as funny as he had been when he came to Orlando.

And by that humid summer morning in 2006, I had noticed a trend. Matt wasn't the only staff member who had showed signs of lethargy and negative emotions on the job. The day-in and day-out, for a lot of staff, especially the single and/or younger ones, left them jaded, bitter, and disappointed. For many of the more administrative staff members, life on the inside was far from the glamour and excitement of the stages, conferences, and media interviews in New York City, Washington, DC, or LA that my particular job description offered.

I'll never be like you.

Matt's words rang in my ears as I struggled to formulate a worthy response to the charges he had inadvertently leveled against me. To him, he was offering a potentially career-killing admission of guilt. To me, I had been exposed as a fraud.

It took a few moments for me to gather my thoughts, but I knew, in that moment, I had my own confession to make. To him.

"Matt, I'm not the goal," I finally said, tears threatening. "I'm not straight. I'm definitely not perfect. And I am still attracted to men. I do love Leslie, and I am attracted to her. I am in love with her. But I've misrepresented myself and my experience of healing if I've given the impression that my life is struggle-free." I took another moment to gather my next words. "I am so sorry I've made all of this seem easier than it is. As of today I won't do that again. Your goal shouldn't be to be like me. Straight isn't the answer. I will be honest when I share my story from this day forward. Thank you for being honest. It will change me."

The conversation with then twenty-five-year-old Matt was longer than what I have shared, of course. And Matt didn't snap out of his funk immediately either. But my admission did help, both him and me. Our honesty was an encouragement to each other. I could see him physically and emotionally exhale. But I also knew it brought up more questions for him. If my story was different than what I often shared publicly, and if I *wasn't* straight, was there hope for him?

This come-to-Jesus moment happened just days before the Thirty-First Annual Exodus Freedom Conference being held that year at Indiana Wesleyan University. I was the speaker on opening night for a crowd of about a thousand attendees. I went into this event with Matt, and people like him, heavy on my heart.

In front of the crowd and with Matt in the audience, I first publicly uttered the words, "I still have same-sex attractions." Prior to that, I'd said things like, "I will never be as though I never was." Emphasis on "was." Was gay. It was a subtle but important distinction. As long as I remained in the "used to be gay" camp, my supporters and colleagues were happy.

A number of people picked up on the different language

I used this time—on the difference between "I used to be gay" and "I still have same-sex attractions"—and some people used my words against me. But there were a lot of people, to my surprise, who found it refreshing. Many LGBT bloggers and pundits also took note of it, and many of them saw it as an encouraging sign that Exodus was evolving. Worst-case scenario, in their minds: I'd made a temporary gaffe that poked holes in the credibility of "change." Best-case scenario: Exodus was showing signs of decline. A few of my most conservative friends, like Tom Minnery, VP of Public Policy for Focus on the Family, even praised me publicly for being honest about the reality that you can't just flick a light switch and turn off gay or turn on straight. He had heard so many others share that they had *walked away from* homosexuality, and he thought that made it sound easy, like you could just quickly turn around and go the other way without any real fight. Rarely did people, including me, who gave testimonies of "change" ever hint that their sexuality might not be wrapped up in a neat little package with a silver bow.

Two years later, I had to make the hard call and lay off Matt because of budget cuts. That, among many other grueling decisions, caused me to feel drained. But I knew beyond doubt that Exodus was where God had me, and going elsewhere was not an option. At that point, I was barely halfway through my tenure as president.

The following six years would be turbulent and

excruciating. Laying Matt off was hard, but I hadn't yet been faced with the hardest decision I would ever make.

I'll be the first to admit: I have prayed one simple word a thousand times in recent months. "Help." Over the past few years, Leslie and I have jumped off one cliff after another in a fight to be transparent and to continually experience and share God's grace. We have lost friends and financial security. But not for a single split second do I regret my decision to close Exodus or the path I've taken since. I have experienced more growth in the past few years than ever in my life, and perhaps equally as important, I've been more honest than ever too.

So here is my true story. My exodus.

CHAPTER 1

GROWING UP CINDY BRADY

"Mrs. Chambers, at your age you must brace yourself for the likelihood that your child will be mongoloid."

The chauvinistic, gray-haired military doctor stood in his white coat in front of my forty-year-old mother, looking through his black-rimmed glasses between his clipboard and her eyes and delivered his unsubstantiated bias that I would be born defective. Mongoloid is, of course, now a painfully derogatory term, but in 1971, society used it to describe people with Down syndrome, people who have three copies of chromosome 21, rather than the usual two.

As if he were scolding her for being pregnant in the first place, he said, exhaling, "I recommend you go to New York and have an abortion." It was two years before *Roe v. Wade*, but abortion had nonetheless been a common practice in New York. "There's no reason to bring this baby into the world at your age and with five other children to care for."

His duty done, the physician ordered her to get dressed,

gave her an obligatory pat on the shoulder and walked out of the sterile and windowless room. My mother was left stunned on the edge of the green metal examination table, staring at the linoleum tiles below her dangling feet.

My beautiful, kind mother cried that day, and she wasn't one prone to tears—she's as strong as a sequoia. I remember her often saying, in her slow, southern drawl, that "it isn't pain that kills you." She taught us kids that almost anything could be done in the midst of pain. Even though it threatens to kill, it never does. She lived through so much hardship, and it made her empathetic and kind to others who were struggling. I honestly cannot remember a time when hard decisions got the better of her.

As always, Mom shared these burdens with my dad. "The doctor believes the baby has a high likelihood of birth defects because of my age," she said, "and he thinks I should have an abortion." My mother never struggled with conveying difficult news. She is as matter-of-fact as they come.

"An abortion? Nah. It will be okay, Mom." (My parents rarely called each other by their first names.) Dad was great in a crisis. Although he was hotheaded most of the time, he seemed to replace his impatient nature with a cool head in the face of urgent decisions. "The baby will be fine. We will be just fine. Don't you worry." With his hand on hers, reaching across the front bench seat of the car, my dad reassured her that they would do what they always had: they would make it.

My parents decided that the doctor was wrong. I'm

not sure his being right was ever considered. Even if their baby was born with disabilities, they would love him. That was my humble beginning and a foundational lesson that my life was sacred. I was wanted.

———⌾———

My mother has the most beautiful soft skin and caring eyes. I've heard more than one of her childhood friends and family members describe her as "the prettiest girl they ever saw." I couldn't agree more. She is beautiful inside and out.

Thirty years prior to finding out she was pregnant with me, my mom lost her own mother. Mom was eleven years, five months, and six days old. Two weeks before Christmas, her fifth-grade teacher received a note from the school office.

"Betty, gather your things. Someone is here to pick you up."

Believing her mother was there to surprise her and take her Christmas shopping, Mom almost skipped down the hallway, pitying the kids imprisoned in their classrooms. Excitement turned to horror when she saw her Aunt Ann's sweet face overcome with grief.

Aunt Ann, a very big woman who was almost unrecognizable without an apron tied around her large waist, hugged my mother tightly. "Your mother has died of a heart attack this morning, Betty. We have to go home." My mom became an adult that day.

While facing life as a motherless eleven-year-old, with

a father whose busy career as a judge prohibited him from being home and a sister whose own grief led her to spend most of her time outside of the house, my mom became the head homemaker. She took care of her older brother, Gene, who was born with congenital issues, which sentenced him to a life of dependence on the care of others. Uncle Gene is amazing, funny, brilliant, and has added life and joy to our family. We wouldn't be the same without him.

That same year, Mom's oldest brother, Junior, got married and moved into the family home. He eventually had two kids whom Mom helped care for as well.

Soon after high school, Mom married a man named Jim and had two children of her own. Jim died in a car accident in late 1950, shortly before the arrival of their second child. There had been a depression, a world war, the loss of her precious mother, and now another heartache. Family and caring for children were what she had known and what she loved. But she needed to make ends meet after her husband died, so within a year my mom got a job at a book store near her home in downtown Knoxville, Tennessee.

Within the course of another year, a friend and coworker named Evelyn insisted my mom meet her youngest brother, Bobby, who was home for a month on leave from the United States Air Force. Mom agreed, and in less than a month's time, on March 16, 1953, she married my dad, Sgt. Robert Lance Chambers. Together they had four more children. Six altogether. And when it was all said and done, they were married for fifty-four years.

More than any of my other five siblings, I was inquisitive and was always asking to hear my parents' stories. And my mom's story shaped my early childhood. She was my whole world.

Whenever fragmented memories of her mother drifted into our conversations, I worried I'd lose her like she lost her mom, but I kept my fears to myself. To speak them out loud, I believed, would bring them to life. But sometimes I became consumed worrying about it. I envisioned life without safety, without laughter, without warmth, without her. But even though I never voiced my fear, my mom sensed my concern and insecurity, and often ended her stories reminding me, "Honey, I asked the Lord to let me raise all of my kids and he said yes."

When she spoke that promise out loud, she gave us both a line of hope on which to cling.

Pam and Patti are my older sisters, respectively twenty-three and fourteen years older. Pam recognized and fostered one of my greatest talents: shopping. We love shopping. She invited me to shop with her locally, nationally, and internationally. Early on I think she took me with her because I could keep up and because whenever she asked whether something looked good on her, I answered yes.

Patti was one of my dearest childhood friends. Where Pam had a family and was both a sister and a mother figure, including me on vacations with her family, Patti was more of a fun, sweet, teenage sister with a hint of mischief and a flair for drama. I remember being three years old and out on errands with Patti. Before seat belts were required, she would swerve on back roads and I would slide from one side of the white vinyl front bench seat to the other.

During an era when walking was far more common, she'd pull up beside a pedestrian on the side of the road and ask them if they were tired of walking. When they answered yes, she screamed, "Then run!" peeling out in Mom's 1973 dark green Impala Coupe. That was Patti.

My brothers, like my dad, were more of a mystery to me. Charlie was twenty-one years older, Bob was eighteen years older, and Fred was only six years older, and I loved them dearly. But our lives never quite lined up. Charlie was married and worked hard and often. He was busy taking care of his own family, but when he visited, he often plopped me on his lap and pretended to be a flying airplane. His thumbs were the controls by which I steered the plane. Other times, he threw me on his back and swam across a nearby pond or took me sailboarding or sailing on local lakes. Bob was the one who couldn't wait to leave the nest and go to far-off places. Though it wasn't quite Africa, he went to school in Tennessee, then Palm Beach, and then Texas, collecting a load of degrees and a wife. Bob was the football star and surfer turned unlikely pastor. He was cool and came into town just long enough to make us all want more. Time with my brothers was good; there just wasn't enough of it.

Fred and I spent more time together under one roof than we did with any of our other siblings. I imagine he probably wanted to kill me far more often than he let on. Living life with little Alan couldn't have been easy. Poor guy. Fred was a Boy Scout, played baseball and soccer, and made his own dirt bike out of pieces he found. In my mind, at least, he was what a real boy *should* be like. Fred was most comfortable around other boys. Fearless and playing hard. He was good to me. If ever there was an ideal older brother for a gay kid, Fred was it.

—————— ✺ ——————

As a kid I loved watching reruns of *The Brady Bunch*. Though I didn't know at that early age that our family was blended, I identified with the Bradys. Our family had six kids too, except in ours there were four boys and two girls. But as the one who was turning out to be quite the gender nonconformist, I might as well have been the child that evened up the sexes in the Chambers Bunch. I was the youngest one ... quite literally in curls.

The Brady Bunch was my first favorite "real people" show. I originally wanted to be Jan, but Cindy was my destiny. Outwardly I might have been the boy who failed to even up the sexes in the Chambers family, but in my childhood mind, I was born a girl in a boy's body, and lived for a decade playing that role inwardly and some-times outwardly. Most of my prepubescent life was spent believing I was a girl trapped inside a boy's body.

I loved trying on my mom's white pumps, and

eventually graduated to Patti's polyblend green skirt and boots. She had a pair of shiny black go-go boots and a pair of brown suede boots that I loved to parade in around the house. The memory of clicking those heels on our hard dark pine floors still thrills me. Our long galley kitchen served as my favorite catwalk. My dad, who had retired from his career in the United States Air Force two years before I was born, must have hated that his youngest son was so feminine. I don't remember being disciplined for that early behavior, which is exceedingly curious to me when I look back, especially knowing how strict and intolerant he was of all things gender nonconforming.

Dad traveled a lot when I was a kid, opening hotel restaurants for C. B. Day, the founder of Days Inn. Both a chef and restaurateur, my dad helped develop the concept for Day Break, their first restaurant endeavor. There were seasons when he was gone for weeks at a time. Sometimes more. One of those seasons when Dad was away, a girl named Kathy moved into our neighborhood. I was four years old, and because it was 1976, I was allowed to roam the neighborhood freely for hours. The good old days. We'd never let Isaac and Molly do that today, even as ten-year-olds in a safe neighborhood.

I was sometimes mistaken for a girl. I had big round blue eyes and long thick dark eyelashes. My mom loved my curls and let my hair grow enough for them to form. Hey, it was the '70s.

One day, I met Kathy and her family, and they asked me my name.

"Alice," I said, coming up with the first female name that came to mind and started with an A. It felt great, though. Like I was living out my inner truth.

Kathy quickly became my best friend. At her house around the corner, I could be Alice without fear of being found out. Time frames escape me, but it feels like Alice hung out with Kathy for a couple of weeks.

Those glorious weeks ended on an early September afternoon. It was close to dinnertime, and I was playing in Kathy's room. The sun was starting to set and I knew I should probably get home for supper, but we were having a great time playing house. I was in the midst of reprising my role as the beautiful teenage sister. Or was I Jill Munroe from *Charlie's Angels*? Can't remember. Nonetheless, in the midst of my performance in the white-walled room Kathy shared with her younger sister, tucked away at the end of the hall with a window facing the front of the house, I heard the doorbell ring and my brother Fred's voice inquire after me: "I think my brother Alan has been playing here."

Kathy's mom replied, in an almost *aha* tone, "Do you mean Alice?"

Fred sighed, probably rolling his eyes. "Yep. That's him."

I panicked and quickly instructed Kathy, who was staring at me inquisitively from between her twin beds with Holly Hobby spreads, to say, "There isn't anyone here. My friend has gone home."

I threw myself into the closet. Kathy was confused

but did her best to lie on my behalf. She was no match for the persistent questions from her mother and my brother. They cracked her like a walnut in a vice.

Kathy's mom asked me to come out of the closet and confronted me, with a slight amount of disgust and disappointment: "I thought your name was Alice?"

I said, "Heavens no. I told you my name was Alanssss."

Cue Fred's sigh and exaggerated eye roll. "Come on Alanssss. Mom is waiting for us."

I wasn't crazy about the name Alice anyway. Sounded too much like a diner waitress from Jersey or a middle-aged housekeeper with a butcher for a boyfriend. Sorry if your name is Alice. I mean no disrespect.

I don't remember what the conversation with Fred was like on our short walk home around the corner, but I can imagine him shaking his sensible ten-year-old head, wondering what he was going to tell our mom.

When puberty set in for me at around eleven years old, the feelings of being a girl and wanting to live as one subsided. I may not have been the stereotypical boy, but I grew to like being a boy and never again thought of my gender as a mistake. My sexuality, on the other hand, was now my main concern. I didn't want to be a girl, but that was little consolation, given the reality that my feelings now indicated I was gay.

CHAPTER 2

ALTER CALLS

"So why are you here, Alan?" Because of the nature of Rick's job, I thought his question was an odd one, at best. He should know why I was there.

I tried to keep my face from showing I had no idea how to answer, even though the answer was obvious. Rick was facing me, our knees about two feet from touching. His office was small, lit by lamps, and smattered with antique furniture, but not in a feminine or even well-decorated way. I wondered whether that sense of masculinity was intentional.

Rick was anything but feminine. About five feet eleven, he had a big face, gold wire-rimmed glasses, and scraggly sideburns that framed his round jowls like carpet runners. Suspenders were made for men like Rick, who had strong shoulders, skinny legs, and a big belly. The faded tan corduroys he wore surely would have given way to gravity had they not been hoisted and supported by his shoulders. The condition of his plaid shirt and boat shoes intimated they spent more time on his body than in his closet. His thinning and receding hair was unruly, and he had an air of impatient condescension. I was intimidated.

I had taken a lot of time preparing for this meeting, had both dreaded and longed for it. It felt like walking onto my high school campus for the first time, like a first date with someone I really liked, like the most important job interview I'd ever face. I wanted these people to love me. I needed them to love me, to accept me. At age nineteen, I was about to share my deepest darkest secrets.

I needed to play it just right. My starched white oxford Polo shirt, starched pleated Polo chino khaki pants, argyle socks, and cordovan Weejun loafers helped cover my insecurities. My coifed, thick, dark brown hair nearly fossilized by Aqua Net Super Hold gave me an added sense of false security. Destined for straightness (that is what I went looking for) or not, my hair would not fail me that day.

Minutes before I walked into Rick's office, I'd parked my white Honda Accord under the large oak trees in a cramped asphalt parking lot made uneven by massive roots. As I approached the door of the ministry, I couldn't help but notice the late-model black Ford Bronco II parked out front. It had an empty gun rack in the rear window, a rebel flag, and a bumper sticker reading "Proud Member of the NRA."

My family's southern, Christian, and Republican roots go deep. One of the family photos etched into my mind is of my maternal grandfather as a judge presiding over a midnight raid where police were dumping illegal moonshine. I knew about the NRA and the good ole boys who were card-carrying or bumper-sticker-toting members. Surely the owner of the truck wasn't inside Eleutheros, the ministry claiming to help people not to be gay. Eleutheros was a member of a larger organization called Exodus International. I knew nothing about them except they were Christian and they helped people like me. Gay people.

I'm not Sherlock Holmes, but now, in the small non-profit office, staring at Grizzly Adams, it took only a few seconds for me to deduce that Rick owned the SUV with the missing gun. He shattered every expectation of what gay looked like. I sat close enough to him that I am sure he felt my tension and smelled the Versace I'd sprayed. As I formulated a cool response to Rick's obvious question, my eyes frantically scanned the square room, looking for the missing rifle. *Is he going to give me a running start and then hunt me out of homosexuality? Is this* Candid Camera? *In a race to the death, will my loafers or his belly ultimately cause one of us to falter?*

"I want to be straight," I finally said. "I want to be normal like my family. I want to get married to a woman and have kids. I want to be here six months and never have to talk about any of this ever again." My skills as a prophet go only so far, apparently.

My answer seemed to humor him. "We'll see what we can do about that," he chuckled. His smile was warm and his comment, though sarcastic, was full of empathy.

"Tell me about your family."

———— ∞∞ ————

Dear God, no. Please don't let this be happening. It was all I could think as my parents recounted their church service to me. My mom had made a typical Sunday lunch: eye of round roast paired with carrots, celery, mashed potatoes and gravy, and cornbread. And butter. We are southern and butter isn't an accessory; it's a side dish. We sat in the kitchen, at the octagonal glass-top table, in the same places we had always sat in the home where we had lived for more than a decade. I had recently graduated from high school and was attending church, but not with my parents. They wanted me to hear all about their service. They had no idea of the nuclear impact of this small talk. I was about to be the proverbial deer caught in the revealing headlights of an oncoming Mack truck.

My mom, who always sat to my right, began, "There was a man who gave his testimony today in church who used to be gay. He was there with his wife beside him. He works for a ministry and is going to be taking it over soon."

I had no idea what ministry she was talking about and wasn't about to risk showing any interest to find out. I could feel my face turn as red as the fresh Tennessee tomatoes sitting on the relish plate in the center of the dinner table.

"He went there for help after years of having affairs with men. His wife forgave him, and she works at this ministry too. He used to work for Jerry Falwell at Liberty University."

My mind was racing. I was the deer. I could smell the diesel of the Mack and almost taste the cold shiny chrome of the truck's grill. Should I be perfectly still, hoping the disaster would be averted by a last-minute swerve? Or should I dart into the nearby woods for cover? I desperately needed to end this conversation before any sense of my secret was discovered. But a glimmer of intrigue and hope kept me in the middle of this dark road of potential death.

My mind raced. I wanted to say something cool without giving anything away. To get them off the subject but not without learning a little more information. A name. The man's name. Then I would run into the thick forest of another subject.

I snapped into a role I had learned to play oh so well. "Gross!" I said cocking my head back like a snake ready to strike. "They let people talk about that in church?"

I was playing a game; it's called Hypocrite. Homosexuality wasn't gross to me. It *was* me. I'd known it since about fourth grade, since the moment I'd connected the dots and realized I was one of *those* people I'd heard about on the playground and at home. A part of me needed to think all things gay were gross. That being gay made me gross. I had been indoctrinated with religious and bullying hyperbole concerning homosexuality and gay people my whole life. Both my faith tradition and being southern, which is nearly a religion itself, taught me this response. To squeeze in to the ill-fitting mold of what was expected of me, my reaction to gay *required* disgust.

Hypocrite is not a fun game. It's hurtful and hateful

and harmful. It's rooted in fear and shame and causes hope and truth and joy to be suffocated by its thorax-shattering death grip. There are no winners in the hypocrite game except damage and destruction, loneliness and betrayal.

But it was a game I had little choice but to play. "Who is this guy?" I asked my mom at the kitchen table. "Is he a member of your church or just visiting?" Turning my attention back to my plate and the comforting mashed potatoes, I waited for my parents to answer.

My dad didn't say much, and his silence on such a topic was odd to me. He seemed at a loss for words. Looking back, I now believe they both knew I was gay, and this was the beginning of their trying to figure out how to navigate such an unfamiliar reality. From that day on, I never heard another negative word from him about gays, effeminate men, or anything of the sort.

Mom filled in the gaps. She laid down her fork and tilted her head ever so slightly toward the ceiling as she thought for a moment. Betty Chambers has a lot of brain under those curly brown locks she's had fixed every Friday afternoon for decades by Roseanne, her hairdresser.

"Let me see. I think he said his name is Rick Hughes," Mom said without turning to look at me. "I can't imagine anyone doing the things he mentioned, but his message was really good. I think you can get it on tape."

Ahh, the promise of 1990—a testimony on a cassette tape. I dreamed of listening to the tape in my car, the only place I was sure to be alone and safe, wrapped in the plush maroon interior like a child in a security blanket.

I could listen to this Rick Hughes talk about how to get ungay. Thank you, Jesus.

Alas, it never happened. I never got the tape. The obstacles were insurmountable. I never figured out how to ask for it or pick it up myself without giving away my secret. But I did stare at Rick's family photo and contact info in the church directory and almost called his house many times.

Only a few months earlier, my brother Fred had called out of the blue and invited me to a special service. "Hey Al"—my family calls me Al—"I want you to come hear a guest speaker who is doing two services at my church this Wednesday and Thursday." No additional information was needed. Fred asked and I agreed. I liked Fred and I liked going new places.

During the course of the service it was obvious that the speaker was telling a story similar to the one my parents would soon hear at their church, but this speaker never mentioned the words gay or homosexuality. I thought I knew what he was talking about, but he never said the words.

The story my parents told coupled with Fred's inviting me to a special service about homosexuality couldn't be a coincidence. Fred must have wondered whether I was gay. My parents must have wondered whether I was gay. Were they talking to each other about it? All this talk about men going from gay to straight, but no one ever asked me whether this was my reality. I'm sure I would have denied it had they asked. Glad they didn't, I went back to my normal life. And by normal, I mean carrying a secret, praying for God to heal me, and heaping mountains of shame on myself every second of every day.

———— ⬡ ————

Shortly after the conversation with my folks around the lunch table, my youth group went on a weekend retreat to Carpenter's Home Church in Lakeland, Florida, about forty-five minutes south of Orlando. The megachurch could accommodate ten thousand people and looked like a lot of other monstrous church buildings built between 1978 and 1990, a sort of churchy spaceship. It was the *Millennium Falcon* with doors and windows anchored to the ground in the middle of an enormous parking lot with named sections, like Disney, but Christian. I think our bus parked in the Shekinah Glory lot.

Dawson McAllister, a curly-haired, middle-aged, loud, engaging-to-youth-but-annoying-to-adults evangelist was the speaker. Dawson was edgy. He seemed to speak teenager fluently. He might have been as old as some of our parents, but he didn't act like our parents. He wasn't afraid to laugh or to say things that made us laugh. He had a way of talking about "our stuff" that made us feel like he was one of us. He spoke to us as if we had brains and were capable of using them. Our defenses were lowered and we were ready to hear whatever he had to say. We trusted him.

Because he had earned my trust, I was able to take a step that changed my life forever. On the last night of the event, Dawson invited several groups of us to come forward to the space between the end of the stage and the front row of the auditorium. He invited those who had never before entrusted their lives to Jesus to come forward. He invited those who were willing to recommit their lives to Jesus. He invited anyone who wanted to be prayed for to come forward. And he invited one specific individual, or at least one specific type of individual, to come forward.

"I want to invite a special person to come and talk to me personally. I think there is someone here tonight who feels they are gay and who believes suicide is the only option to curb their pain." He briefly paused. "If that is you, please come talk to me. I want to tell you something."

As subtly as possible, I looked around to see if anyone was staring at me. How had he read my mind so completely, so accurately? I was sure he had said my name aloud. To my relief, no one was looking. When the final invitation was given, most every kid in the building left their seat and slowly made their way forward. Finally, I reached Dawson, who was off by himself in a dark corner waiting inconspicuously for me.

I looked him in the eyes and whispered, "I'm the gay kid." The words were awkward in my mouth, foreign. It was the first time I had said them out loud.

"Great! Come with me. Let's talk over in the back corridor away from the crowd."

Making our way to the small secluded hallway leading backstage, I followed the curly-headed man resembling

Weird Al Yankovic and thought, *I'm so grateful I won't be seen with him.* I also wondered if he wanted to get me to a quieter place where he could explain just how awful I was. Or maybe he didn't want me to miss any of the things he was planning to tell me to do in order to get right with God. My mind raced, my palms were sweaty, and my heart was pounding out of my chest. I considered running out the back door.

Reaching our destination, we sat criss-cross on the rust-colored carpet between two shiny white walls, and Dawson said, "Okay. So, you're the gay kid."

"Yes, sir," I said with embarrassment. I felt sick admitting it. What had I done? Why didn't I just stay in my seat? How would this end?

"Great," Dawson said with the same exuberance he seemed to have in all situations. I had no idea what was so great about being the gay kid. Didn't he have any other word or response? Everything is definitely not great. But he continued, "I just want to tell you one thing. I want you to hear these three words and remember them."

Steeling myself for the condemnation sure to come, I listened to him say something without understanding a word. Like Charlie Brown's squawking teacher. His words didn't match my expectations. I had to ask him to say them again. This time, laying down my expectations, I heard.

"God loves you." He looked intently at me to see if I had comprehended the magnitude of his words. When I didn't reply, he said them again, "God loves you." Still no response. "God loves you."

Finally, I asked, "Did you misunderstand what I told you? I am *gay*."

He chuckled. "I know. And God loves you."

Dawson spent twenty or so minutes with me sitting on that rust-colored carpet. He told me about verses in the Bible that promised that there was hope for a kid like me. Most of his words escape my memory, but I will never forget what it felt like to hear God loved me while the words "I'm gay" swirled in the air over our heads. I had exhaled one truth and inhaled another. God loved me. I was breathing. There was hope. I wanted more.

Dawson wanted me to tell my youth pastor. He said he would call my youth pastor in two weeks to see if I had told him. To me it was a threat. No way was I going to tell my youth pastor; I had heard his derogatory remarks about this or that looking gay or how gay something was. They were never said from a stage or with contempt, but the thought made me feel unsafe. I knew my youth pastor would never understand. No way. Dawson saw and quieted my fear. He asked if it would be okay to call my youth pastor and have him suggest a counselor. I agreed as long as he promised not to tell my secret. He promised.

My youth pastor called me into his office one Wednesday night after youth group a month or so later. Apparently someone from Dawson's team had called. My pastor asked me a few questions. I told him it wasn't a big deal, just some family issues I was trying to work through. He didn't press me but did give me the card for a counseling center in Orlando where I could get the help I needed. To this day, I am unsure whether he knew more than he let on. We never talked about it again.

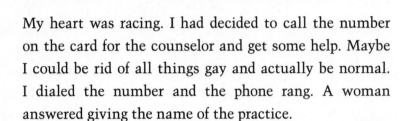

My heart was racing. I had decided to call the number on the card for the counselor and get some help. Maybe I could be rid of all things gay and actually be normal. I dialed the number and the phone rang. A woman answered giving the name of the practice.

"I'd like to make an appointment to see a counselor."

"Of course. What is your name?" Gloria, as I came to know her, was lively and sweet and sounded like she loved her job. I instantly wanted to tell her everything. Instead, I simply made an appointment and hung up. This was long before everyone and their brother had cell phones (my brother Charlie actually did have one), and I had taken advantage of a rare moment when our house was empty to make the dreaded call. After which I dropped into a chair and settled into the realization that I was going to tell someone, *local, in my hometown,* about my struggles. The news coursed through my body like an instant laxative.

The day of my appointment, I got cold feet. "Hi, Gloria, this is Alan Chambers and I need to reschedule my appointment."

"These things happen. When would you like to come in?" I chose another date and time and assured her I'd see her then. She was so nice. She deserved a name meaning joy if ever anyone did. We hadn't met, but I was sure she'd get to heaven.

"Hi, Gloria. It's Alan Chambers again. I just realized I have classes the morning I scheduled my appointment. Can we make it for next Thursday in the afternoon this time?"

Her nonjudgmental "Of course" followed. "When would you like to reschedule?" I gave her another date.

As I stood in the phone booth outside the bookstore of Valencia College facing into the thick woods behind the school, I promised Gloria and myself I would keep this appointment.

Exiting the phone booth, I walked slowly, which is rare for me, across campus to my afternoon English composition class, passing friends who called out to me. I simply nodded my head, thinking only about my big, fat gay dilemma. Though moments before I was sure I'd keep the appointment, five minutes of walking to class was all it took for the fear of uttering the words "I'm gay" to set in. By the time I took my third-row seat next to my friends Chris and Kelly, unzipped my brown suede backpack, and pulled out my book and notebook, I knew I would cancel this appointment too.

I called later in the wee hours of the morning after my parents had gone to bed and simply left a whispered message: "Hi, Gloria, I'm not going to be able to make my appointment this afternoon. I will call to reschedule." Hanging up the black rotary dial phone, I put my face in the palms of my hands, closed my tired eyes, and breathed in deeply. *It will get better. I'll pray it goes away. God can do anything.*

More than a month went by. For every day I was confident I wanted to talk to someone, there was another day I was scared to death to say the words "I am gay." I made and canceled appointments acting like that deer wrestling with the decision to stay still or run. Poor Gloria bore my annoying ritual like a champ, never letting me hear even a hint of frustration. Exasperated with myself, I finally asked her point blank, "Do you counsel gay people? I mean people who are gay but don't want to be gay? I am gay, I think, and I absolutely don't want to be. Gay, that is."

"Oh honey," Gloria said as if on the brink of tears. "Of course we can help. One of our counselors meets regularly with gay men. But there is also a ministry in town that specializes in that called Eleutheros. Maybe you could call them."

I was calling from my part-time job in the takeout room at Red Lobster. Alone and using the wall phone next to the cash register, I leaned on the counter of the takeout window. I grabbed a notepad and scribbled the name as I'd heard it, *Allutheross*, along with the phone number. (I later found out the people at Eleutheros joked about how to pronounce the ministry's odd name. They pretended it was a man named E. Luther Ross. And, in public, to disguise it, they simply referred to it as The Ranch.)

Ignorant of Greek, I furrowed my brow and thought, *The Lutherans have a ministry for gay people? Interesting.*

I immediately called and made my appointment with Eleutheros and was scheduled to speak to a counselor who happened to be the executive director of the ministry as well. I figured he would be safe. As I understood it, he was like me. He had been gay. The ministry ended up being the same one my parents had spoken of. The counselor ended up being Rick Hughes. I figured it was fate.

Eleutheros was indeed a ministry serving Christians with same-sex attractions that provided encouragement and support as they surrendered their struggles to the lordship of Jesus Christ. That particular ministry was a member of the worldwide group known as Exodus International. Eleutheros had been around since 1982. It had been in my own back yard, only a few miles from my home and church for more than half my life, and I never knew.

I felt relieved. I also felt angry that no one had ever mentioned such a ministry. I was determined to keep this appointment.

Now, on September 12, 1991, here I was nearly knee-to-knee with a suspendered Rick Hughes, telling him about my family and how normal they are. "Mmhmm," he muttered as he scribbled notes. "There's no such thing as normal. Tell me about your relationship with your dad."

"I don't have one."

"You don't have a dad?"

"I have a dad. He and my mom have been married almost forty years. We love each other, but I don't have a good relationship with him. He likes sports and I don't. He has a bad temper. We are so different from each other.

I've never wanted to be like him." I was calm and matter of fact. This topic made me anxious.

"Ahhh. Typical. Most guys who are gay have the same story." Rick began to share what he understood to be my problem. "You have unmet homo-emotional needs. Your homosexuality is rooted in your desire to be loved, affirmed, and accepted by the same sex. It's not about sex at all. It's about unmet needs. Get those met and your desires will diminish."

HALLELUJAH! This isn't even going to take six months. I'm going to get my needs met and get outa here. It sounded oh so simple. I was sitting straighter already. I fixed my starched white oxford Polo shirt, sat back into the 1960s-style doctor's office chair, propped my elbows on the armrests, and crossed my legs. Smiling, I said, "Let's get started."

It was the beginning of a twenty-two-year relationship with Exodus. Eleutheros felt like home. The people of Eleutheros felt like family. The building itself was a small, no-frills, four-room office suite plus a bathroom. It had been one of those 1950s L-shaped roadside hotels converted into offices. The front door opened to a sidewalk bordered by plants separating it from the parking lot. It was older and offered nothing fancy but had a warm and welcoming feeling. Despite his gruff exterior and confusing love for hunting, rifles, and the rebel flag, Rick was kind and fatherly. He had a loving wife, Gwen, who frequented the office. She was a computer whiz and worked at a local college. The receptionist, Jim, was a thirty-something man from Alabama with the sense of humor and demeanor of a night-shift waitress at a truck stop. He also was trying to be ex-gay. He smoked like a chimney, wore red Converse high-tops, and called me honey. I liked them all a lot. They welcomed me and loved me. They challenged me, and showed up for me consistently for years.

It seemed all roads had been leading me to Eleutheros, to Exodus International. This community filled a deep craving I had to belong somewhere. Anywhere. Authentically. Now I did. I knew I would stay a very long time.

CHAPTER 3

E. LUTHER ROSS

I gave Rick Hughes and Eleutheros a good six months. I had always found school difficult, but I became a faithful student of the Eleutheros program, which I'd hoped would change me from gay to straight. Eleutheros, a Greek word, translated means freedom from bondage. Gay = bondage. Straight = freedom. At least that was the idea.

Here's a little background on the organization.

In 1982, a single Christian woman named Gayla Durance, in her thirties and pursuing a master's degree in social work at the University of Central Florida, founded Eleutheros. Her mission was set when she saw the response to a question she posed to a room full of gay men she was studying. "If you could take a pill guaranteeing you would be straight by morning, how many of you would take it?" Every man raised his hand, and Gayla started her journey and a support group at Calvary Assembly of God, a megachurch in Winter Park.

Originally named Be Whole, the ministry was wisely renamed Eleutheros in 1984. During the 1980s, ministries were popping up all over the country aligning with Exodus, many of whom named themselves with Greek words found in the Bible. They offered "freedom from homosexuality through the power of Jesus Christ."

Eleutheros didn't charge much money for their services, and if someone couldn't pay, then that was that. They weren't in business for money. The organization subsisted on a shoestring budget, provided by a handful of faithful donors—most of whom were personally connected—as well as a few daring churches like Orlando Christian Center, pastored by the now infamous Benny Hinn.

The fees of Eleutheros were nominal: fifty dollars a week for two group meetings and one professional counseling session. It wasn't much. Being nineteen, a full-time student with only a part-time job and with parents who didn't know my secret, I found even the nominal fees to be a challenge at times. The reality was that in 1991, fifty dollars was a week's worth of entertainment, including the gas it took to get there. When I shared my dilemma with Rick and other leaders, they assured me I would never be turned away for lack of funds.

As intimidated as I had been by Rick that first day, I came to like him quite a bit. My weekly counseling appointment was with Rick, who was a licensed counselor, but the fact that we shared a common story made his advice and support even more valuable to me than his degrees. Most of our sessions in his small square office were simply spent talking about my childhood, how insecure I'd always been in my own skin, and why I felt attracted to guys. On occasion, I absentmindedly found myself looking for the missing gun. We talked about my relationship with my mom, my dad, my siblings, and my peers. We talked about how I had internalized negativity, clung to anything shame based, and blamed myself for not being good enough at anything related to masculinity. Like sports. And posture. And inflection. The appointments were less about my being gay and more about my being given the space to talk through realities of my life that I wouldn't and couldn't share with others.

I cannot imagine what it's like to be in the witness protection program, having to look over your shoulder every second of every day. Always knowing there is someone after you. But Rick helped me see that I had felt something like a witness protection victim feels. I relentlessly hid my feelings, my attractions, and my shame. I covered my tracks, pretended, played a role, and never stopped fearing being found out. It was traumatic.

My two support groups were a men's accountability group and a group for adult survivors of childhood abuse. Both groups were segregated by gender, and for what seemed to me to be a good reason. Most of the women appeared wounded and fragile and deeply fearful of men. Most of them had horror stories of sexual and physical abuse. At the time, I just thought that was what caused them to become lesbians.

My accountability group was made up of eight to ten men, most of them single. A couple of the guys had been married, and one was still married. I was paired with an accountability partner, and we checked in with one another several times during the week. We were given the task and the freedom to ask each other questions aimed at encouraging honesty and good behavior (which meant not having sex with men, real or imagined). Monday nights we broke off into pairs and went through an explicit checklist. The structure of this group resembled Alcoholics Anonymous. It wasn't quite, "Hi. My name is Alan and it's been three days since I fantasized about a man," but it was close. Very, very close.

1. Have you been to any known gay hangouts?
2. Have you paid for or been paid for sex?
3. Have you masturbated?
4. How many times?
5. Have you been honest?

I will never forget the first time I read those questions. Paid for sex? Been paid for sex? Who are these people? I would never do that. I mean, I didn't know where to even look for such a thing. I thought questions three and four were funny. At nineteen, I wasn't sure my weekly number would fit in the small space allotted for the answer.

The group for adult survivors of childhood sexual abuse was larger. There were fourteen of us crammed into a small ten-by-ten-foot office along with a desk, bookcase, and a hodge-podge of other furniture I longed to discard or at least rearrange. The room often got very warm and uncomfortable. We had a non-gay-related curriculum and workbook we used. The combination of warmth and being taught lessons out of a book made me tired. I've always been an early-to-bed kind of guy, and though I liked the group, I fought to stay awake each week. I easily could have snuggled up to a fellow participant and gone right to sleep—until it was my turn to talk. I loved when it was my turn to share. The other guys always seemed interested in what I had to say and always had a kind response.

One particular night, I had news to relay, and I sat up straight on the edge of my chair to tell it. I felt oddly giddy by this point, lightened by the announcement.

An hour before this very group meeting, I had been sitting at home in our family room recliner after dinner. Before I could stop myself, I blurted out, "When I was nine, an older neighborhood boy experimented with me sexually." I said it abruptly and matter-of-factly, like I was telling them I planned to have cake for dessert.

Mom sat in her chair at the glass-top table to my left, and Dad was in his spot on the couch to the right of me, ready to watch *ABC World News Tonight* with Peter Jennings. I had been staring out the glass doors in front of me. It would soon be dark.

I rubbed the palms of my hands on my jeans in the milliseconds it took for the silence to be broken.

"I guess that means I was molested."

My dad turned, looked me in the eye, and both casually and definitively said, "No, you weren't." In hindsight, I think he might have thought I was joking. (I'm not sure why, but maybe he hoped I was.) In the moment, I was shocked at his denial, and my deep-seated hurt and anger toward him bubbled to the top.

"Yes, I was!" I shouted and felt a rush of tears.

I looked to my mom for help as I bounded out of my seat and rounded the corner toward the door to the garage. I had to get out of there. Right before I slammed the door, I heard my mom say, "Bobby, he doesn't think you believe him. Go after him."

My dad caught me just as I was getting into my car. I could tell he was sorry before he ever said a word. I knew I had shocked him with my disclosure and that he reacted before he knew what he was reacting to. He said, "Son, I'm sorry. I just didn't know what to say."

We went back in the house and talked a little more. Reluctantly, I told them more details. "I don't remember exactly when this happened," I offered. "I just remember what my room looked like." My parents listened in silence. They knew I was upset and, aside from my dad's off-the-cuff remark, they were handling it very well.

"I still had my twin bed, and it was during the time when I had that blue bedspread with the Star Wars characters on it." I calmly recounted the important aspects of the encounter to my mom and dad. "I didn't understand it all. He said he wanted to 'try something,' and then closed my door and locked it. It was painful, but quick. He swore me to secrecy, insinuating that I was complicit and would get into trouble. It happened only that one time, and honestly, I don't think he had harmful intentions. I think he was a stupid kid trying to figure out what felt good, at my expense." Then I told them that I was going to counseling.

It was incredibly difficult, but also a relief, to tell my parents where I'd actually been sneaking off to on Monday and Tuesday nights. And I could tell they were relieved to understand more about me. Still, I didn't admit that I was gay, and I wondered if I might be able to keep that secret forever. If Eleutheros helped me become straight, my parents would never have to know the whole truth.

Rick and the others in the group thought telling my parents had been a step in the right direction.

"I hope so," I said. "It felt good and important to tell them. I mean, it has, in some ways, really plagued me. There was even a period of about two years when I stopped going to the doctor because I was afraid I had AIDS because of that afternoon with my neighbor," I confessed to my new friends. It was cathartic and freeing to have a place where I could share my secrets with people who understood. What a gift it was to me.

"You thought you had AIDS because of that incident? Wasn't he basically a kid too?" Ron, a sixty-three-year-old husband, father, and grandfather asked. Ron and the other guys cared about me. They wanted to help me. I think all of them felt like they could spare me the horrors they'd seen and experienced in their gay lives.

"When I was ten, I heard AIDS was God's judgment on the 'homo-sexual.'" I said it with the same emphasis I'd heard it come out of the southern preacher's mouth. "And I thought just having gay thoughts and masturbating meant I was bound to get AIDS. I thought I could give it to myself. But I was also worried my neighborhood friend might have given it to me. I didn't know how someone got the virus. From the way I heard one televangelist explain it, 'AIDS is God's judgment on gays just for being gay.' Because of that, I thought if I went to the doctor for any reason, he would find out I had AIDS and everyone would know I was gay. I couldn't risk being found out, so I stopped going to the doctor."

Larry, a thirty-year-old professional with hair like David Cassidy sat looking at me with his big brown eyes and said with the utmost care, "Oh, Alan. I'm so sorry. You do know better now, don't you? That you can't give yourself AIDS and that a loving God wouldn't ever give anyone a disease?"

"I do know better now." I couldn't help smiling remembering how naive I'd once been.

———— ◌◌◌ ————

During my first six months at Eleutheros, I would have gone every day if something had been offered. I enjoyed the relationships and the ability to be honest. It was the only place I felt relaxed, and yet it was also a place held together by tension. I often found myself stopping by or calling the ministry for no reason other than because I could. These were the only people who really knew me. But as time went on, I realized I was part of a subculture whose members were in some sort of limbo. We didn't identify as gay. We couldn't honestly identify as straight. We were ex-gay-ish. We were strugglers. Was this all there ever would be?

One afternoon on the heels of a counseling session with Rick, in which I had admitted to some pretty serious self-loathing, I walked into the lobby and saw my friend Daniel, who had the next appointment to see Rick. Daniel was almost twenty years my senior, from North Dakota, and all about laughing and having a good time. He liked me in a way that felt brotherly. I liked him the way I liked my older sister, Patti. Daniel could tell I was feeling like crap as I puddled into the waiting room chair beside him to collect myself before I left.

The Eleutheros waiting room had a huge window, but the hundred-year-old oak trees hovering over it prevented much sunlight from coming through. The thin metal blinds, though open, added to the overcast feeling of the room. I sat staring out into the parking lot, on the verge of tears.

He had spikey blond hair and ice-blue eyes, and in a thick Minnesotan accent, he said, "You look like you need to have some fun." He wasn't making an observation; he was giving an order. "John is having people over to his house Friday night. You have to come." John was also about twenty years older than me and so nice. He was a member of First Baptist Orlando, a church with about ten thousand members. He often told me it was full of gay people, which was shocking to me at the time.

I knew it wasn't going to be just any party. I knew Daniel and John hung out with real live gay people who didn't want to change, who seemed to have no problem with being gay. Daniel, like so many guys I met at The Ranch, saw being gay as sinful and Eleutheros as a type of evangelical confessional, where he could do penance and settle the tab with God once or twice a week.

But Daniel was right; I needed fun. And his invitation suggested something I'd never considered before. Being gay could be fun. I knew that gay people were fun. They weren't all miserable and awful and deviant like society had taught me. But I'd never thought of myself that way—as actively gay. Maybe I was ready.

Daniel scribbled John's address on a piece of paper and reiterated how much I was going to love his friends and how much fun I was going to have with them. He seemed elated to be the one to introduce this sheltered Southern Baptist boy to a whole new world.

John lived across town, and I was late getting to his house. By the time I walked in and met a few people, they were all getting ready to get into some cars and head "out."

"Come out with us, Alan," said a very handsome and successful dark-haired man, also named Jon, but without the *h*. Jon and I had talked for only a few minutes but acted like we were old friends. "You can ride in my car.

C'mon, you'll have a blast. I will bring you back whenever you want. We can leave if you are uncomfortable."

I got into Jon's shiny new car. He was an executive for a major car company, and they'd set him up with a top-of-the-line black sedan with black leather seats and darkly tinted windows. I found out we were going to The Parliament House, Orlando's oldest and most notorious gay bar, and it felt like I was riding in style straight to hell and in the devil's car. But I was dying to go — to the bar, not hell.

As we drove what felt like forever, about twenty minutes, I stared out the window and wondered what my parents would say if they found out. I was six months into my quest for straightness, and I was also well aware that going to The Parliament House was not going to help me achieve my goal of going straight. I wondered what the people at Eleutheros would say. Would I even tell them come Monday night? What must God be thinking? The old fears of getting AIDS by osmosis or from casual contact resurfaced. I was nervous and excited. Scared and oh so ready.

"So, you have a boyfriend," I said turning toward Jon as he drove. I was curious about this handsome new friend. I was curious about boyfriends. And anything having to do with gay life. "Yep. Greg. He's a waiter. We've been together for a couple of years." I'd get to know Jon a lot better and Greg just a little bit. They were the first gay couple I met. They lived in a nice, normal house that Jon owned. I couldn't believe I actually knew a gay couple.

We pulled into the dirt parking lot at the iconic 1950s style hotel and bar.

"Isn't Jon a hunk?" Daniel was goading me into saying something revealing out loud about my gayness and feelings for Jon. He could tell I was enamored with the uber-confident and successful, unapologetically gay Jon without an *h*. Jon was the first gay man I'd met who hadn't ever questioned being gay. He challenged me greatly. His very life caused me to think a lot about what I believed and why I believed it. Could gay be normal? Could I ever be like him? Could he ever like me?

The crunching of sand and pebbles under our feet competed with the pounding of my anxious heart. I was exhilarated. This was fun-scary, like standing in line the first time I rode an upside-down rollercoaster at Busch Gardens. The guys were aware of my unease and kept telling me how great it was going to be. If the cars in the parking lot were any indication of the number of people inside the place, it was packed. I could smell the Drakkar Noir cologne from well outside the front door.

We reached the entrance and my friends instructed me to just play it cool. I was after all only twenty and not of legal drinking age. There was a chance I wouldn't get in. My stomach was in knots. My heart beat so fast I felt lightheaded. I was trying not to lock my knees, knowing I'd faint if I did. I would not fall and get dirt all over the cream-colored Gap shorts I'd ironed perfectly.

"If they ask for your ID, just tell them you left your wallet at home and look pretty," Daniel whispered in my ear.

Jon was now acting like he was my date and protector. "Have your money out and hand it to them like you've been here a million times," he said with his hand resting between my shoulder blades.

I didn't have any trouble getting in. I was a preppy kid and younger than the others, but more than anything, I was gay, and gay was all you needed to be to get in. My eyes met the eyes of more people that night than ever before. I didn't even have to talk with people to speak the language. Our eyes told each other everything, and we knew this bar was a safe house.

I pulled open the double doors leading to the main bar area and dance floor. The music thumped, the sound waves nearly visible. It was dark, but lit with a blue light. A big rectangular bar to my left and a crowded dance floor to my right. I followed the guys through the mass of people across the parquet dance floor, where we found a couple of round high-top tables. It was our base camp for the night.

"Rob is working tonight. The drinks and view are going to be good," Daniel said. My friends laughed like schoolgirls talking about the home-team quarterback.

Rob was dressed in tight dark jeans and a white linen shirt that was bloused and unbuttoned to his naval. He was tan with dark hair. "What can I get you, handsome?"

"He'll have a gin and tonic." Jon took the liberty of

ordering for me. I liked his assertiveness. I was looking for someone to lead me. Maybe Jon and I would fall in love and I could be a happy househusband.

Throughout my life, lots of people had assumed I was gay and had made fun of me for it, but these people didn't make fun of me; they *wanted* me. I felt like I had been handicapped my whole life but the moment I walked into this place I felt normal. I was gay and I was one of them. The cement foundation of fear and rejection crumbled, just a bit, every time my eyes met with one of those guys in the bar. What I believed was the worst thing anyone could know about me, being gay, was not awful. It was celebrated. Everyone's gay! It was a party, and I partied.

I laughed and drank and looked at guys until the wee hours of the morning when all of us decided it was time to go home. Driving back to John's house, John with the *h*, I chewed gum to conceal the smell of alcohol and started piecing together the story I'd tell my parents if they asked where I'd been—and planned my next visit.

"Can we go again tomorrow night?"

"I think somebody had a good time. Welcome to the life, Alan." Everyone took great pride in the part they'd played in breaking the preppy Jesus freak out of his closet.

———— ∞∞∞ ————

Telling my Monday night accountability group that I'd been out at the gay bars Friday, Saturday, and Sunday nights got easier over time. Their disappointment mattered to me, but it was a small price to pay for the amount of fun I was finally having. I was going to counseling and support groups three days a week and out to the gay clubs three nights a week. Wednesday had become my day of rest. I quit church. There was no point in going to a place where they would hate me if they knew who I really was: a gay man trying to be straight and torn between two worlds.

One of those Wednesdays in May 1992, the Chambers brothers—Charlie, Bob, Fred, and I—got together for lunch. Because of our age differences and life situations, we hadn't all hung out before, just the four of us, and I left the reunion full of food and belonging. Since Fred was on his lunch break and headed back to work, he asked me to take the leftover pizza to his first wife, Kim, who was home with their four kids, who were all ages four and under. I was happy to do it; besides, it was on my way.

I arrived at Fred and Kim's house happy. The tension of my alternate worlds and personas quieted momentarily in the security of family. Once disconnected by age and station, my brothers and I had laughed and we had remembered. Together. We purposed to do it again. Consumed by contentment, I knocked on the screen door and waited on the porch for Kim to answer. I could see the dark great room and Kim tiptoeing toward me. She unlatched the screen door, greeted me with a warm smile, and welcomed me in as she had a million times before.

The house was quiet. It was one of those cherished moments when all four kids were napping at the same time. That's why she was tiptoeing. Kim and the house were comfortably dressed. Pleasantly arranged, yet showing signs of the four lives temporarily at a standstill in another part of the house. I was still standing just inside the front door with the pizza box in hand when Kim, compelled not to waste a moment of the priceless quiet, jumped into a conversation that shattered my serenity.

After a little conversation about lunch, brotherhood, and how rare the moment we'd all just shared was, she segued with all the confidence and poise of a seasoned journalist. "Fred and I have wondered whether you like girls or guys."

What? Did I hear her right? She knew me well and would know I was lying through my perfect white teeth if I said anything other than guys.

Fidgeting with my keys in one hand and the large pizza box in the other, I shifted my weight from one foot to another. And then I said it. "Guys. I like guys and I am going to counseling to deal with it."

"We thought so," Kim interrupted. "It's okay. We know a lot of guys dealing with the same thing."

Once the pizza box was properly stored in the fridge, there were no distractions. With Fred at work, it was just Kim and me sitting across from each other, not so differently from the way I sat when I talked to Rick in my counseling sessions. I told her I was going to counseling at Eleutheros. She knew all about Eleutheros because there were a number of guys, maybe a few women, who had attended or were attending Eleutheros who also went to their church.

"Are you going to church anywhere?" She knew the

answer and didn't leave time for me to make excuses. "You should go to Discovery tonight with Fred and me."

I'd been to Discovery Church once before when I listened to the guy who never mentioned the word gay but alluded to having been involved with a man. I had been uncomfortable with their liveliness, especially in worship. It wasn't Southern Baptist. Charismatic was what they called it. It was emotional and expressive, with only a thin veil of order. But going to gay bars, with their freedom of expression and emotions, had since forced me to loosen my grip on tightly bound behavior. I was now up for anything. "Okay, I'll go."

"Great. Be here at five tonight and you can ride with me. Fred will meet us there after he gets off from work. Afterward, you can ride home with him and talk more about all of this." The thought of riding home with Fred and talking about "this" frightened me, but it was inevitable, I supposed.

To my utter surprise, I saw several people I'd met at Eleutheros that night at Discovery. Within a matter of seconds, I knew there would be no hiding at this church. I would definitely go back.

As I flitted in and out of groups huddled around the auditorium before the service started, greeting people I knew, the security of being known that I had experienced earlier in the day at lunch with my brothers resurfaced.

Discovery was close to Disney property, and a lot of singers and dancers from the parks made Discovery their church home. To the gay man and the lesbian woman who had a yearning for God and a tendency toward drama, music, or artistry of any kind, Discovery was a beacon of hope. When the worship singers came out onstage, I could tell several of them were just like me. Looking through the crowd of people, there were quite a few of me there that night. It was kind of a holy gay bar without the booze or Miss P—the resident drag queen at The Parliament House.

It was surreal sitting in the congregation with my brother and sister-in-law knowing they knew my lifelong secret. I'd been there all of fifteen minutes. It felt a long way from the recesses where I'd shared my deepest, darkest secret with Dawson McAllister.

Weeks flew by. My schedule of three days a week at Eleutheros and three nights in the bars continued. But I added Discovery's Sunday morning and Wednesday evening services to the mix. Being in a community where I was known and where my relationship with God was celebrated more than anything else was sweet and life-giving. And it made the gay bars less attractive to me. I was growing weary of focusing on myself. I was growing weary of indulging my problems and pleasures.

It's not like I was having sex. At this point, I was still rather innocent sexually. I was underage and drinking too much and thoroughly enjoying the attention of others, but there were several mornings that I barely dragged myself out of bed after staying up most of the night going to clubs. I wasn't proud of my life and I wanted to change. I was still going to Eleutheros. Still reporting in on Monday nights to my accountability brothers. Still trying to see which life would win out. Though I was only twenty, I imagined what life would be like at fifty and didn't want to be living in this kind of turmoil.

"Alan, I don't care if you have been out all night long doing God knows what," Kirk told me one Sunday. "No matter what, make sure you get to church on Sunday mornings."

Kirk had become like a younger father figure to me. We'd met for a Ministry Time—kind of like a pastoral counseling session—met for lunch a few times, and gotten to know each other better. He was the farthest thing from gay. He was married with children, but he understood me. He understood my wrestling with God. "This is your home. We want you here. Never forget that."

I'd told him so much. Our first long conversation, about five hours, was spent with my face buried in his shoulder, heaving as I sobbed through the revelation that I ached for male love and affection like a starving child in Africa aches for food. He wasn't ever grossed out or offended. He cared.

One Sunday night, to please my parents, I went to their church with them. Sunday night was probably my favorite of all nights to go to the bars. They were always packed. I told my friends I would meet them there about 8:00 p.m. On the way out of church, I said goodbye to my folks, saw Rick Hughes, and even stopped to talk to him for a moment. Having put in my time for good behavior, I patted myself on the back and eagerly headed to The Parliament House.

This was the pre-cell-phone era, when plans were plans and you trusted people would be where they said they would be. I stopped at a pay phone on the way to call Jon to make sure he and the others were still planning to meet me at the club. No one answered and I deduced they must be en route. By now I was known by the staff at The Parliament House, so I walked through the doors not the least bit concerned about being carded. Inside, I took a few laps around the perimeter of the bar looking for my friends, who were nowhere to be found. I settled into a prominent table in the bar just inside the entryway with a view of the double glass doors where everyone entered, ordered a drink, and worked hard to appear at ease. I watched anyone and everyone who came into the bar.

Rob, the bartender, wearing the same white shirt unbuttoned to his navel and tight dark jeans, made me another amaretto sour. I was now a seasoned bar veteran and knew what I liked. Glancing covertly at the doors every time they opened, I hid behind my glass and waited. And waited. And drank. My friends never showed. It was pitiful. An hour later, my pity party was interrupted.

"Alan."

I looked up from the bottom of my glass, wondering who'd said my name.

"If you choose to stay here the rest of your life, I will love you."

Okay, I thought, looking over both of my shoulders to see who was speaking.

"What you think is *good* is the enemy of my *best*. There's nothing that can make me love you any more or any less. But if you trust me, I will show you my best."

There was no one there. How many drinks had I downed? I was pretty sure it was God talking to me.

"How in the world did you get in here?" I was baffled by his presence and his monologue. Baffled he'd bother with a reprobate.

"You'd be surprised at the places I go."

I raised my glass and nodded in acknowledgment of the comeback. I whispered, "Touche!"

People were everywhere, but no one else heard the voice. The Swedish band Army of Lovers was singing "Crucified" as my high-top table in the corner moved to the beat of the sacrilegious music that had become a guilty pleasure. Miss P, the sixty-year-old drag queen, was holding court in the room just around the corner. The Parliament House wasn't a place where God "should" be, but God was there. I suspect he's always there. I found him to be just as real that night calling me to himself as he had been one morning when I saw him in the baptistery of First Baptist Winter Park fourteen years prior—the morning I decided to give my heart to him at age six. I learned a lot about God that night in the gay bar.

"God," I prayed, "I'm so tired. I don't think this life is good. I'm miserable. I don't want to be here. But I am so tired and I can't get up. I don't have the emotional strength to leave. I need a sign."

Out of habit, my eyes turned toward the opening glass doors. Two single people, a man and a woman, walked in. I knew them instantly. They were from Discovery. They were new friends of mine. They saw me, smiled as if they had been planning to meet me there, and walked over.

"We just got out of church and were driving by and saw your car, and God said you might need some company," they said with all the confidence of people who regularly talk to and hear from God.

I was at a loss for words. I didn't want to be alone. I wanted to leave the bar but had no ability to move. Frustration and a sort of despair anchored me to my seat. My gay friends had abandoned me, I had decided, and my new friends offered me assurance that God hadn't. In reality, all of my gay friends had real jobs and had decided to take the night off to rest before work the next day and couldn't reach me to let me know. But the possibility that they'd stood me up had given me some time to think and, oddly, to talk to God about where to find my worth. That conversation with him was one that changed me forever, causing me to realize that he would never leave me and that like Kirk and these new friends, God was not hesitant to accept me fully.

"Do you want to get out of here? We paid the cover charge and we'll stay if you want. But we just wondered if maybe you wanted to go get something to eat and talk."

I finished my drink. Then I got up and walked out of

The Parliament House with them. And I've never been back.

Hindsight is twenty-twenty. I knew a fraction of the "here" to which God was referring, the physical location of my body in that gay bar, but I didn't know all of what God truly meant by here or that there was more to know. I don't regret walking out that day but neither do I regret any part of the nights I spent finding a part of myself in those bars. The gay bar scene ended up being a necessary part of my story, and God was there the whole time. It fueled many dysfunctional patterns in my life at the time. When God said he would love me even if I chose to stay *there* for the rest of my life, he was talking to and about my innermost being. My emotional and mental condition was utter chaos. The *there* was a place where I was desperately working to find peace and acceptance, somewhere, anywhere. I was working to reconcile my faith and sexuality, and *there* I was forcing everything. The gay bar itself was not the problem. It was just the symbol of my turmoil.

What I later learned, and hold on to, was that God's best for me was not simply to end the struggle between gay and straight, to force me to choose. His best for me wasn't one or the other. His best was for me to rest in him spiritually, emotionally, and physically. His best was yet to come.

I had one more round of gay self-discovery.

I moved out of my parents' house on my twenty-second birthday and into an apartment with a friend I'd met at Eleutheros who also went to Discovery Church. Neither of us identified as gay but we were open with one another about the challenges we faced and our deep struggles trying to live the straight and narrow.

Not long after moving in, I discovered my apartment complex's jacuzzi was a late-night hookup spot for the gay men who lived there. It was at that jacuzzi that I was hit on for the first time by another guy who clearly wanted to have sex with me. Prior to this, my gay experiences had mostly involved hanging out with other gay friends. But this was the real deal. Scared to death, I quickly made an excuse to leave and ran to my apartment, crying all the way. But I went back again the next night and another guy hit on me, and this time, I didn't run back to my apartment. Instead, I went back to his apartment with him.

I settled into life on my own, a life that wasn't yet yielding the changes I'd hoped for in my same-sex attractions. I was working at Eleutheros during the day, honestly believing what they offered was good, and yet hiding the reality of my night life. I worked a second job waiting tables. The restaurant was close to my apartment and in an area of town where a lot of entertainment types lived—a lot of gay men. It was a good place to "come out." I hid my Eleutheros life in a closet.

I spent about eighteen months living this double life. The gay bars had been a cakewalk comparatively. Going to bars seemed nothing like being sexually active with men I didn't know. I didn't have intercourse, but I still was at risk for STDs. Plus, emotionally, I was doing something I knew was far from good for me. I never left those encounters feeling like this was the life I'd wanted.

I think the tension of still going to Eleutheros yet not getting any straighter and living as a gay man, at least at night, actually helped me to mature. I came in one night after an encounter with a guy feeling dirty and used and like a user myself. I immediately got in the shower and wept as I scrubbed my body trying to cleanse myself and remove the smell of a cologne that I can't stand to this day. I didn't want to feel this way anymore. I prayed for help to move beyond this season of my life to a God who didn't condemn or reject me. I knew I could bring this to him and trust him with it. And together with God in that shower at 3:00 a.m., I determined, chose, not to go to the jacuzzi anymore.

I realized that my gay feelings might never go away, and that was okay. It had to be okay. Though I never acknowledged my secret life to anyone except two of my closest friends, I was acknowledging all of it to God. He knew everything. And I was learning firsthand that God's love is unconditional and unchanging. I came to stand on the truth that salvation is irrevocable and that I could truly be who I was and live how I wanted to live without the fear of losing my relationship with Jesus or the fear that I'd never had one in the first place. I learned to make decisions based out of that security rather than the fear of rejection that religion had once instilled in me.

Funny, that important piece of the puzzle had first come to me in my favorite gay bar the night God showed up and told me he loved me as I was—*as I was*—which, that night, was drunk. The same revelation was now playing out in my heart and mind, even as I tested the boundaries and limits of God's love and acceptance while testing out anonymous sexual partners. His boundaries, I concluded, were limitless. His grace was sufficient. Many years later I would teach this at Exodus, telling an audience in 2012 that even when they found themselves lying next to someone with whom they'd had sex but not taken the time to exchange names, to repeat this truth: "I am the righteousness of God in Christ." It was this revelation that led me to make better choices.

CHAPTER 4

RESOLUTIONS

A lot happened in my early twenties. Years I should have been going to college and learning a skill, I spent learning about life. I found Eleutheros and gay bars and the jacuzzi. Then I left the gay bars and the jacuzzi and stayed at Eleutheros. I even started working there full time. And after I attended my first Exodus International Conference in 1993, I told my parents the real reason I was involved at Eleutheros and they, mercifully, became two of my biggest supporters.

In 1995, I also became involved as a leader within the greater Exodus International organization as a member of their annual summer conference team. I served as the emcee, a role given to people who could handle a crowd. It was a role I had requested and was granted, even though the leadership of Exodus didn't really know me all that well. Emceeing the conference for the first time at Point Loma Nazarene College in San Diego meant rubbing shoulders with the board of directors, elders of the ministry, and the most infamous of speakers and leaders from the movement. It was at this conference that I became close friends with Dennis Jernigan, John Paulk, and others well known in Exodus circles. I was honored to have the job and to meet the people I had deeply admired from afar.

During these early twenty-something years, I left my Southern Baptist roots and joined Discovery Church, where I learned to be transparent about many things, including most of my struggles with homosexuality, with a group of people who loved and accepted me all the more because of my honesty.

"To struggle" was the verb most commonly associated with homosexuality within the ex-gay subculture. To accept the gay label was to associate with a lifestyle God didn't ordain and couldn't bless, yet to adopt the label straight seemed pretentious and disingenuous. We felt that the word struggle communicated the truth of it all. I was, and we were, struggling between two worlds. Trying not to be gay was one big excruciating struggle, because it is impossible. Trying to be straight is equally impossible. Such attempts are pretty much always motivated by shame and fear, unfortunately sending too many gay Christians into dangerous and secretive lives that most openly gay people would never lead.

The best thing I ever did was stop trying to be either/ or. It was during this transition in my life from childhood to adulthood that I did attain a deepening level of acceptance for myself. I decided to be celibate, which provided me a peaceful respite and sobriety, and to focus solely on knowing God, which was different than fearing God. I chose to follow God because I wanted to and could, not because I had to. And I realized God loved me completely. Unconditionally. Always had. Always would. No matter the direction I chose. I was free to choose my path, and I chose to pursue God and see where he led me.

———— ∞∞∞ ————

"Martha and I hope y'all have a safe New Year's Eve and that 1996 is the best year of your lives. We love you all. Now get out." Clark Whitten had a way with words. This was only the second time I had heard him speak in person, and he was as brashly endearing this time as he'd been about a year before, when he was the guest speaker on a Sunday morning at Discovery Church. He had shared his personal testimony and demonstrated a gut-level honesty as he talked about grace. In the spring of 1995, I learned he'd become the new pastor at Calvary Assembly of God, one of the oldest churches in town and one of the country's original megachurches—and coincidentally where Eleutheros began in 1982. I was drawn to him, and on New Year's Eve in 1995, after I heard Clark Whitten preach again, I became a member of Calvary.

The New Year felt like the right time to make changes in my life, and church was the most fundamental part of my existence. I dearly loved Discovery. It was a place that welcomed me when I was trying to figure out who I was—gay or straight or somewhere in between—but by 1995, most people my age had left or gotten married and moved away. For a time, I settled in and built quality relationships with people quite a bit older than and different from me, but rather than stay and become the lone single twenty-something in a group of forty-somethings, I opted to leave. I was lonely there.

Plus, I was excited to learn about grace the way Clark Whitten preached it. He and Calvary Assembly seemed to beckon me like Jerusalem did for many Jews and Christians. I needed to go there.

Shortly after the New Year's Eve service, my good friend DJ invited me to a home fellowship group. The first night I went to the Thursday night fellowship group, it was a full house of about fifty people. I found a place on a couch across from DJ. The event had already started when a beautiful girl came in. Her body language communicated she knew she was late and wasn't a fan of being the center of attention. She sat down on the carpet in front of DJ, directly across from me.

She was well dressed and looked successful. She intrigued me. She reminded me of a couple of actresses in movies I'd watched. She was like the character Elizabeth Perkins played in the 1986 movie *About Last Night*. She was Stockard-Channing-esque. She was interesting, a bit aloof, secure, and I wanted to get to know her.

From that night on, whenever I saw her, I tried to get her attention, making jokes that my friends laughed at, and I watched for her to laugh, but she didn't. I stood in crowds where she was and hoped she would acknowledge me, but she did not. I was exceedingly perplexed and determined to be friends with the mysterious girl, whose name, I soon found out, was Leslie.

A short while after I started attending the home fellowship group, I ran into DJ, Leslie, and another friend at my favorite restaurant in Winter Park one Sunday after church. The atmosphere bolstered my confidence. We were on my home turf. It was a typical sunny day on Park Avenue, Winter Park's smaller and more charming version of its Manhattan namesake. Their table was snugly nestled into a corner between two plate-glass walls overlooking the patio and the park.

I took leave from the friends I was lunching with and approached DJ's table. "Hey, you guys. How's lunch? Church was great today, huh?" I smiled, overconfident in my charm.

"Hey, Alan, you know Laura. Have you met Leslie Paull?" DJ is the epitome of southern charm and manners. I did know Laura. And of course, I also knew of Leslie, and now she would know me and have to engage with me. Ha-ha!

"Excuse me, sir," the waiter said, foiling my plan and drawing all eyes to himself. He needed me to move out of the tight space so he could deliver their lunches. In my heart I was kicking and screaming, but calmly I acquiesced. Once again Leslie and I didn't get a chance to talk.

I begrudgingly bid them farewell. In a last-ditch effort to raise her eyes toward mine, I said to Leslie, "Nice to meet you, Leslie," but she was more interested in helping the waiter rearrange the table-scape to make room for their food.

"Argh," I grumbled under my breath as I walked away disappointed and went back to my table and lunch party. At that point, I didn't realize I had feelings for Leslie. I didn't know I was as enamored with her as I actually was. But I did know I desperately wanted to get to know her. When they finished their meals, Leslie and Laura left to shop in the Ann Taylor store next door. DJ came over and joined me and the people I was eating with. I didn't understand why Leslie didn't come over and say goodbye. And I couldn't understand why she was so resistant to being friends with me. *Good grief, this girl is tough,* I concluded. *I'll try harder.*

Because I worked at Eleutheros and had been on local television to share my testimony, at that point, I wasn't shy about my story—minus the eighteen months I'd spent infrequently visiting the jacuzzi. I'd become the go-to guy at Calvary for questions about gay stuff. It never ceased to amaze me how many people came out to me at church, and how often. Whether it was them personally, or a son or a daughter or an aunt or an uncle or a mother or a father or their daughter's friend or their son's teacher, there was a seemingly endless slew of people in church who either were gay or knew and loved someone who was gay. People with all sorts of sexual "issues" found their way to me as well. One woman talked to me about her relationship with her husband, who wasn't gay. They hadn't had sex in ten years. Another woman regularly called the church wanting to talk about her incessant masturbating. They sent her to me. I was called when Briana, a transsexual church member who had a five o'clock shadow *and* breasts, used the women's bathroom and scared Sister Rose. Although one of my goals was to become a pastor to people like me, I had no idea what I was in for, even in this unofficial capacity.

One Sunday evening after church, an elderly man stopped me in a quiet hallway.

"I'm glad you're here, Alan," he said. "I'm eighty years old. I've been married to my wife for nearly sixty years. I have more children and grandchildren than I can keep up with. I became a Christian before television, almost before Ford invented the Model T." This man was only a bit older than my dad. "I am happy. But—and this is the first time I've said this out loud—I knew I was gay when I was a teenager. I'm so glad you're doing what you're doing. I knew there were others like me. But in my day, nobody wanted to talk about such things. I'm glad people can talk to you. I would've liked to talk to someone. It got a bit lonely at times. But God is good and I've lived a great life with my wife. We've been happy and will be until God takes us home." It was a heartbreaking story, but a beautiful one too. It encouraged me in more ways than one: it made me realize that a happy, long-term, monogamous, heterosexual marriage was possible even for a gay man, and it also made me believe I had a ministry, that I was doing good in the world.

Soon the youth pastor at Calvary offered me a position

as a high school Sunday school teacher. It took only a couple of weeks for one of the longtime associate pastors to protest to his immediate boss, who wasn't Clark, the senior pastor. The two of them put their heads together and decided they couldn't let someone with a past like mine, even though they had no clue about my actual past, teach high school kids. What would people say? A gay dude, even if he says he's celibate, might take advantage of one of the teenage boys. How's *he* going to teach them to be a man of God? Of course, no surprise here, they didn't talk to me. They conveyed their decision to my youth pastor friend, their subordinate, and he, in turn, fired me, with much anger and disappointment—at them.

At the youth pastor's urging, I appealed to Clark, who was becoming a friend. Clark, still new and learning the politics of Calvary, apologized profusely, decried the decision, and asked me to wait it out with him. He promised that he would vouch for me and that if he had anything to do with it, I would get my job back. It was the first time, but certainly not the last time, that I would sense in Clark a willingness to fight alongside me and for me. I realized he was both my pastor and my ally. Without saying too much, I knew he was battling old guards and systems. He might have been five feet six, but in my mind he was eight feet tall and one of the mightiest men I'd ever met.

I don't know what Clark said or did, but I do know the pastor who had started the whole mess apologized to me. He told me how much he supported me and my work and that he was just trying to avert a scandal. After all, he had been a part of the church for years and knew a thing or two about scandals.

During the back-and-forth at Calvary about whether I would be a Sunday school teacher, I was still heavily involved in the college/career group, and still deeply enraptured by Leslie Paull. It was amazing how much time I spent thinking of her and how often our paths inadvertently crossed.

One afternoon, while sitting in a salon on Park Avenue during my monthly hair appointment, a lady came in ranting and raving about a rollover accident she had just seen not far away. We were all concerned, because rollover accidents aren't exactly common in Winter Park.

It was a Thursday, and that meant my home fellowship group would meet in the evening, which meant that I would see Leslie. I arrived early as usual and chatted with other type-A early birds.

Garrett, one of the leaders and the owner of the house where we met, said, "Did you guys hear what happened to Leslie? Apparently she was in a rollover accident today and totaled her car. She's okay, but she had to go to the hospital for stitches."

"Oh no!" Kelly began to cry. "I had a dream last week that Leslie was killed in a rollover crash. When I woke up, I started praying for her. I've been praying all week. I was going to tell her tonight to be careful. Thank God she is okay."

I was stunned by Kelly's story, by the power of prayer, and I was deeply concerned for Leslie. I found it a little strange that I had been in the salon and heard about all of this earlier. It was a connection point—albeit an admittedly odd one—and I couldn't wait to share the connection with Leslie.

CHAPTER 5

LESLIE PART 1
FRAMES

If you happened to catch me driving Isaac and Molly to school in the minivan, or running to the grocery store, or walking our overly friendly dog, Beau, most likely you wouldn't think a thing about me. Beau is an eye catcher, and fellow dog walkers often comment on his unusual coat and are curious about his breeding. When out walking with my husband, it's not so different. Alan's blue eyes are striking and he is stylish, yet it's something else entirely that draws their attention. Sometimes they know; sometimes they think they know. Sometimes they look at me for more information.

Since our engagement, others have been interested in Alan and me as a couple. Are we real or a fraud? Recently, I've sensed a few more inquisitive looks coming my way. Who is this girl that's married to a man who is gay ... or was gay ... or whatever?

As a good friend once said, Alan is the picture and I

am the frame. The analogy was a compliment. Frames, whether humble or ornate, can be works of art themselves and worthy of observation. The drama of my story doesn't begin to compare with Alan's, but I know that humans have a propensity to be drawn to simplicity and goodness and stability and kindness and commonality. And those are the ingredients of my life. I am content in the reality of my frameness, especially considering how well matched I am with my piece of art.

I remember thinking as a teenager that my life would be very different from my mother's. Strangely, it has ended up being both very much like hers and very different indeed. My mom is a part of nearly everything I do—the way I clean house, do laundry, grocery shop, garden, raise Isaac and Molly—but the fact that I caught the attention of a man whose sexual attractions tended toward men has added a few twists and turns my mom never had to navigate in her life with my father. That and having a husband who talks about our sex life with Anderson Cooper and Barbara Walters on national television in between sips of coffee.

———————— ∞∞∞ ————————

My parents were only a few months shy of their forty-ninth wedding anniversary when my dad passed away in 2013. Mom and Dad grew up, met, married, and raised my two younger sisters Erin and Allyson and me in Fresno, California. Their commitment to each other and their wisdom in raising their three daughters is baggage

I carry with me today. Carrying personal baggage has gotten a bad rap. I look at personal baggage the same way I do actual luggage I carry on trips: a beautiful necessity that tells a story. Would you ever go on a trip without luggage? Knowing Bob and Sue Paull and what they carefully packed into my life's luggage explains a lot about me and ultimately about my life with Alan.

Mom never earned a college degree, but she is the wisest woman I know. Very little escapes her scrutiny, especially when it comes to nature and people. Like a lizard warming itself in the sun, she stretches toward people with the life-giving commodity of conversation.

She had a knack for knowing things about my friends and me, things I never noticed. She sensed my growing rebellious attitude as I hung out with one friend. She noticed when another was kind to my face but rallied friendship troops against me behind my back.

I could tell that my sixth-grade teacher, Mrs. Maddox, the "Mad Ox," who often wore a sensible green polyester pantsuit, didn't care for me. She often called me out. "Why can't you stop talking? Are you chewing gum again? Why can't you sit still?" Convinced I was a bad kid, I told my mom I thought my teacher didn't like me. I expected Mom to tell me I was being silly and that maybe I should try harder to be good in class. Adults were known allies of one another.

Instead she said, "You're right. She doesn't like you, and she doesn't know what to do with you." She paused and carefully chose her next words. "It's not all your fault. You have a strong voice. When you talk out of turn in class, you *will* get caught. Your voice will reach the teacher even if your friend's doesn't. But your ability to be loud encourages your friends at swim meets. They hear you when you cheer for them. A strong voice is a good thing—it's powerful. Just be careful with it indoors and in class. And stop chewing gum. You'll get cavities."

About my dad. It's nearly impossible to put my dad's words into dialogue. With us, he didn't say much. He was known to *hurrumph* and *ugh* on occasion. He let out long slow breaths, almost whistles. He scratched his inner ear with the key to his truck. He unfailingly sneezed two short sneezes in quick succession—*achoo-achoo!* He laughed with his tongue sticking slightly through the middle of his teeth and with his whole body, but he never talked about his successes. What we heard from Dad was, "Lubjoo," his squished-up way of saying "I love you." We heard him quip, "Let's go, Shaush [or Teedywheet or Snickerdoodle]," as he stood behind the starting blocks at our swim meets and called us each by our nicknames.

My sisters and I grew up swimming competitively, and we did pretty well. We practiced before school and after school and had meets on the weekends. Mom and Dad were at every swim meet, but they didn't run up and down the pool deck yelling, "Go, Susie, go! Go, Susie, go!" as other parents did. Instead my mom packed the ice chest full of good things like cantaloupe and finger jello, and my dad was the head timer, all dressed in white with a stopwatch in his hands.

Fresno is wrapped in the arms of the Pacific Coast and Sierra Nevada mountain ranges, and our family vacations were weekend camping trips. My dad pitched a four-man canvas tent while my mom set up the campsite. Even in summer, we slept in sleeping bags with our next day's clothes under our pillows so they would be warm enough to put on when we awoke. Dad slept outside, guarding his girls at the door. Mom cooked bacon and eggs for breakfast on the Coleman stove as coffee percolated, their scents filling the air. From our experiences camping, we learned some of life's greatest skills, like putting wiggly worms on hooks, splitting a sunflower seed with our teeth, and squatting to pee without getting our jeans wet.

Except for the people in my life—my friends and coworkers and church leaders—my twenties were unremarkable. I was twenty-seven, single, sharing an apartment with a dear friend, and coaching swimming. Life had become pleasant, stable, but a bit aimless when I got a call about a potential job.

"Hey, Sessie! It's Nellie." Nellie was my college pastor's wife. Sessie was what their children called me when they were young. They'd lived in Fresno for a number of years but were now living in Pasadena. It wasn't unusual for her to call.

"Have you got a minute? I want to run something by you."

"Sure. What's up?" I said, settling into the corner of my roommate's couch.

"I've told you about how I've become good friends with Jamie Hershiser—you know, Orel's wife—he plays for the Dodgers." It was 1993 and I knew of him, as did anyone who even sort of followed baseball in the late '80s and early '90s. "Well, they need a nanny, and I thought you just might be interested. It's a full-time job offer. You'd live with them, and they'd need you to start in late August. What do you think?"

What did I think? My beat-up Toyota pickup truck with more than 140,000 miles, no air-conditioning, and a host of problems lay near death in the parking lot below. There were a couple of boys I'd cared for, but no relationships. I was coaching three different swim teams, but perpetually short on cash. The security I knew from my parents mixed with perfect timing made the adventure imaginable.

"Can I give Jamie your number so she can call you?"

"Do it," I said, realizing everything was about to change.

I met the Hershisers for the first time on my way to Romania for a six-week missions trip, where I would use the Bible to teach English. Although the meeting was technically a job interview, it felt more like friends getting together for coffee. We sat in their living room on two matching couches that faced each other and chatted for an hour. Jamie sat across from me with her feet companionably tucked underneath Orel's leg and ate a banana she'd grabbed from the kitchen. I liked them immensely. Being an introvert and knowing some people judge a book by its cover often left me vulnerable. I was insecure about my cover. It was plain and unattractive. I felt okay about the contents, but I never liked the cover. The bulky cable-knit white V-neck sweater and Bermuda-style jean shorts left me top and bottom heavy. My compacted curls and white Keds were the only small things on my body. I had borrowed a friend's mascara, but there was no point in trying to cover up my freckles. My face, which showed every emotion and turned red at the drop of a hat, made wearing blush unthinkable. On my ninth birthday, my mom and grandmother took me to get my ears pierced, so I put in my small hoops hoping they would help my otherwise frumpy-dumpy appearance.

That same grandmother had had a stroke three days before my interview, and I'd left her in her hospital bed. She couldn't speak, but I knew she wanted me to go on my trip.

I whispered, "I love you, and so does Jesus," kissed her cheek, and said goodbye. She passed away while I was in Romania.

Jamie and Orel offered me the job, and three weeks after I returned home from Eastern Europe, I moved from Fresno to Pasadena, embarking on a path that would be a bizarre yet wonderful mix of ordinary things like doing laundry and grocery shopping, and extraordinary things like flying on the Cleveland Indians' team plane with the players and their families to the World Series. I would take their boys to school and see Kevin Costner dropping off his girls.

As much as I knew my life wouldn't be like my mom's, I knew my job with the Hershisers was more than a job. I loved it and the family, and I strongly sensed that it was leading me to an important yet totally unknown destination. One with its own mix of ordinary and extraordinary.

CHAPTER 6

LESLIE PART 2
COME TO THE TABLE

When I first met Alan, I avoided him. My life was busy, full. I couldn't imagine adding anything to it, let alone the commotion that was sure to accompany him. What I saw in him wasn't negative; he looked like a ton of fun. He was the life of the party—even if there wasn't a party, even if it was just a group of post-college single people studying the Bible on a Thursday night. He talked to anyone and everyone. One minute he was at the center of the smart, stylish, and cutting-edge conversationalists. The next he was with the group of guys talking about sports or the girls in the corner who longed to be noticed by the group of guys talking about sports. It didn't matter whether there was more than one group; he was at the center of all of them at the same time. I liked him, but just being aware of his presence kind of wore me out. He reminded me of my friend Michael.

Michael was one of my best friends. He was strikingly

handsome, hilarious, and larger than life. I was honored he chose to be friends with me. He made me feel good about myself as a girl. He regularly made me laugh until my face hurt or until one of us got the hiccups.

One such time, we were sitting around a fire pit playfully singing "Kumbaya" when one of our friends said, "Throw your faggots on the fire." She was only thinking about a faggot as a bundle of sticks, and though I wasn't acquainted with anyone who was openly gay, I pleaded with her never to use the word in such a way again. It was one of the very few times the issue was highlighted, and it was more about a generational gap than opinions and beliefs about someone's sexual attractions. What I didn't know then was that those little instances where seeds of the idea of homosexuality planted themselves in my mind happened over and over again in my life. I know now that God was subtly preparing me for the life I would soon choose.

Michael and I Christmas shopped together. He held my hand, and yet it was perfectly platonic. I thought, *I should like Michael. He's broken up with what's-her-name and is available,* but I never did. For me, he was too much of a good thing. Eventually, he married someone else, and I was thrilled for him. We hung out less and less, but one night a group of us went out to dinner and dancing, and he introduced me to a friend of his, Brian. Brian and I danced and I liked it a lot. It was attraction at first sight.

I'd been working for and living with the Hershisers in Pasadena for a couple of years, across the street from the Huntington Library. The 1920s house that Jamie and Orel had restored was magnificent, and I loved that it was just down the street from where Spencer Tracy lived with his wife (not Katherine Hepburn) and two children. The main house had four bedrooms, if you didn't count the maid's quarters that eventually became the family room. Fine china and crystal glasses were stored under the staircase and secured with putty in case of an earthquake. In front of the pool house there was a fountain that shot up a stream of water that could keep a golf ball bobbing for hours if you placed it just right. I could have been swallowed up inside the grandeur, but the house was a welcoming reflection of Jamie and Orel—solid, beautiful, engaging, full of wondrous surprises and warmth and laughter.

Much like the two nannies who had preceded me—who arrived from Bird-in-Hand, Pennsylvania, in homemade skirts and traditional Mennonite caps and left with their hair down—I arrived wearing a dumpy-frumpy sweater and jean shorts and was in the midst of my own transformation. Jamie wore her femininity like a mink, and it inspired me. She was beautiful, soft, attractive, and all the while practical. She gave me the courage to try on my own brand of femininity. I lost weight, discovered that a little makeup softened my freckles, and Mac blot powder did wonders with my shiny red face. I began to wear mascara, and with a little money in my pocket, I had discovered the joys of Marshalls and TJ Maxx.

I was wearing my first little black dress the night I danced with Brian. I was in my late twenties, and it was the first time I felt even the slightest confidence in my femininity. Being attracted to someone who might be feeling the same way, and simply *feeling attractive*, was a new and welcome experience. While Brian told me about his dream to be married and open a bed and breakfast somewhere in the hills of California, he gently chewed a piece of gum, which accentuated the strength of his jaw.

Later that night, in the quiet of my room, I had no trouble placing myself into his dream. I could see it: the ten-bedroom rustic inn fitted with every modern convenience. Stone fireplaces. Claw-foot tubs with endless streams of steaming hot water. Beautifully crafted quilts and thick feather pillows. Me serving warm, fragrant cinnamon rolls and Brian bringing the horses around for the couple in the Carriage House Suite. After a week of sweet dreams, I confessed my feelings for Brian to Michael. He had already guessed I had a crush on his friend.

He looked at me with a slightly anxious expression on his face. "Leslie, I have to tell you something about me and about Brian," Michael started. "I met him at a group I've been going to—well, I went to it a lot before I got married. It's an Exodus group. Have you heard of Exodus?"

"Nope," I answered, not really interested in where he and Brian had met.

"Exodus is a group for people who are Christians and

who have homosexual feelings but don't want them. It's for people who don't want to be gay."

"Ooookaaaay," I said, the realization of what Michael was saying slowly sinking in.

"I've had those feelings for a while. Brian has them too. I love my wife and we're happy and I don't want to be gay. Neither does Brian, but I thought you should know. Brian thought you should know."

Without saying so, he left me with the impression that Brian was still interested in me and would call. For the relationship that was flourishing in my head, this was an unexpected speed bump. I had to tell Jamie—immediately.

"They're gay?!" she gasped.

"Yeah. Well, no. I don't know." I had no idea. She had been sitting in the corner of the couch wrapped in a blanket reading the newspaper. She let out a slight squeal, flung the blanket over her head, and the newspaper flew to the floor. We giggled through our lack of understanding and discomfort. Here I was in my first foray into being comfortable as a woman, and I ended up attracted to a guy who was attracted to guys. Awesome!

Questions about Brian hovered all day but didn't take form until later that evening. Lying in bed that night, rather than thoughts of homemade cinnamon rolls and horses, other thoughts and questions surged through my mind.

I knew nothing about gay or homosexual realities. No one I knew ever talked about such things. There was a guy I swam with who I had thought was gay, but he had a girlfriend, so, I'd figured, he couldn't have been. A couple of guys at church were sweet and better dressed than most, but they were Christians. Certainly they wouldn't be gay. There were rumors about the girl's softball team at Fresno State, but I didn't know any of them and didn't really think about them. These thoughts disappeared into the recesses of my mind for years, but my attraction to Brian stirred them to the surface. Could a guy be gay and have a girlfriend? Were those guys at church gay? Could a gay person be a Christian? Could a man who was sexually attracted to men marry a woman? Could I be that kind of woman? Did that thought freak me out? Should it freak me out? Somehow I wasn't freaked out.

Alone in my two-bedroom apartment over the Hershisers' garage, contemplating this strange news, I turned on some music. But I should warn you: I'm a bit of a geek, musically. While my sisters were cool and listened to Bon Jovi, the Cranberries, U2, and the Rolling Stones, I preferred John Denver, Amy Grant, Steven Curtis Chapman, and my dad's folk albums, like the Chad Mitchell Trio and Peter, Paul, and Mary. I owned every Christian album B. J. Thomas made, and I was currently listening to Michael Card's *Joy in the Journey* album. The third track is "Come to the Table." In this song, Card sings about how God welcomes to the communion table all who believe him and "accept as their own" the tokens of the bread and the wine.

For he's come to love you and not to condemn
And he offers a pardon of peace
If you'll come to the table, you'll feel in your heart
The greatest forgiveness, the greatest release

Listening to that song, I believed it. I believed it all. For myself and for others. All were welcome at Jesus' table, even me. Even Michael and Brian. There were no more questions about whether gay people could be Christians. There was only the truth that Jesus loved us and gave his life for us. Nothing else mattered.

The crush lasted another week or so, and I never saw Brian again. I'll never know if he had any real interest in me or if he ever opened his bed and breakfast. He was so nice, it's hard to imagine him alone, but I don't know if he ended up with a wife or, being in California, a husband. Though he was not much more than a speed bump in my life, he slowed me down long enough to realize that all, including gay people, were welcome at Jesus' table and that realization changed my entire life.

———— ∞ ————

After I had been working with the Hershisers for a couple of years, Orel signed with the Cleveland Indians. The Hershisers didn't want to move to Cleveland, but for the family, the commute from LA was simply too difficult. It was a long flight with a three-hour time change. Orlando, Florida, crazy as it seems, was a good option. The agency that represented Orel was downtown, spring training and family were close by, and it was a short flight with no time change to Cleveland.

We moved to Orlando in August of 1995. Meeting friends proved difficult because my schedule was hectic. The Indians played into October that year, losing the World Series to Atlanta, and my days off were limited to Sunday and Monday. I think Orel and Jamie felt sorry for me, so they introduced me to one of the guys who worked for the agency that represented Orel.

DJ invited me to his church. I was familiar with the huge mirrored building, having seen it from the freeway, but I thought it was a hospital. I slipped in through a side door as the three-hundred member choir, which was larger than the church I attended as a child, opened the service in song. They wore mauve robes that didn't quite match the ushers' maroon sports coats and were a bit more enthusiastic about worship than I was accustomed to. It was an Assemblies of God church, and I felt like the only person in the room who didn't have my arms raised and wasn't swaying back and forth with the music or mumbling strange words just under my breath. I looked over both of my shoulders for the quickest escape, wishing they had red lights on the floor leading to the nearest exit and a nice attendant to remind me the closest exit was behind me. Sitting next to DJ, desiring friendship, I stayed put. The pastor rose from his seat onstage, where twenty or so other pastors were also sitting, and stood at the wooden pulpit that was almost as tall as he was. He began to speak. He had a Texas accent, and said "'umble" instead of "humble." I don't remember what Clark Whitten preached, but I was drawn to him. I sat in my pew, which was neither mauve nor maroon, but rather a dusty sort of rose, along with three thousand other people, and knew by the end of the service he was my pastor.

DJ invited me to go with him to his fellowship group of mostly single and working twenty- to thirty-year-olds who met on Thursday nights at a home and studied the Bible. Knowing I needed friends, Jamie graciously and enthusiastically encouraged me to attend. It quickly became a welcome weekly event for me. I felt comfortable knowing DJ, who was well liked, and I seemed to get along especially well with the guys, because I could talk about sports.

One lazy afternoon, I was flipping channels on the TV and landed on a religious station. Two guys were being interviewed, and something about them caught my attention. The show was called *Coming Out*, and they were telling their stories about "coming out of their gay lives." They referred to Exodus—the group Michael had mentioned. The host had a swath of golden blond hair and resembled Rudolf's elf friend Hermie. His name was Victor. The other, with dark brown curly hair and piercingly blue eyes, caught my attention. His name was Alan.

So when Alan and Victor walked into the Thursday night Bible study the very next Thursday, I recognized them immediately. I thought, *There are those two gay guys from TV*. Then I resumed chatting with a friend about baseball.

CHAPTER 7

LESLIE PART 3
YOUR KIND OF GOOD

Unlike David Letterman's top ten, the list of qualities I wanted in a husband had only two items. Of course, being a Christian and having a good sense of humor were inherent in me and therefore necessary qualities I was looking for; good looks were relative, and friendship with guys was never an issue for me. It was the part where they liked me as *more* than a friend that had proven problematic. So my list wasn't about *characteristics* I found attractive. I found Paul Newman and the star quarterback of our high school football team attractive, but I didn't want to be in a relationship with either of them. Attractions are wonderful and I couldn't have been in a relationship with someone I found unattractive, but without my short list of qualifications, attractions had become meaningless to me. Instead, as a nearly thirty-year-old single woman, what I longed for was someone who (1) liked me first and (2) was strong enough to tell me no. I wanted to be pursued by someone I could trust. As it happened, I married the first guy I was attracted to who also pursued me and proved himself trustworthy.

━━━❧◦❧━━━

Alan and I became friends on a forty-foot fishing boat. It was the first time (and so far the last) that either of us had fished in the deep, open seas. A group of six friends—three guys and three girls—planned the trip and chartered the boat off the coast of Key West for three days. I was dating one of those guys.

John actually was tall, dark, and handsome, and one of the leaders of our Thursday night fellowship group. He was raised in the South, so his manners, which were as charming as his drawl, were unnerving and yet also exciting to this California girl. I had never needed boys to open doors for me, thank you very much, but the first time he placed his hand gently on the small of my back and ushered me through the automatic sliding doors of our grocery store, I was smitten; I couldn't help it. Walking just behind me, he guided me past the floral department, past the fruits and vegetables, past the meat counter, and to the bread aisle. We were on a mission to retrieve hot dog buns. Mission accomplished, he skillfully strode in front of me and paid for the buns. I couldn't believe it when he asked me out.

After each of my first few dates with him, my mom asked, "Has he kissed you yet?" I was twenty-nine and still told her everything. She has a way of asking questions that is simultaneously endearing and infuriating.

"Not yet," I sighed.

"What's the matter with him? Is he gay?"

I'm not prone to emotional overreactions, especially disrespectful ones, toward my mother, but I hung up, instantly and forcefully. *Of course,* I thought. *Someone finally wants to date me and Mom thinks he's gay.* Was I so mannish, or unfeminine, or strong, or forceful that my mom figured I'd attract only gay men? But somehow I internalized that idea. *Only a guy who likes guys would like me,* I thought. It was feeding time at the Insecurity Zoo apparently.

Mom didn't ask the question again, but a week later I was finally able to answer her. He had kissed me, and Mom and I were both relieved. But three months later, and on the day of our fishing trip, our relationship was drowning.

John and our other shipmates immersed themselves in the fishing. They fished in the morning and in the afternoon and throughout the night. Alan and I fished, but we also ate and slept and talked to each other. Without crowds to please, I started to get to know Alan and to enjoy him. He listened as I talked about my floundering relationship with John. I knew Alan was funny in big, crowd-pleasing ways, but on the boat I found him to be funny in small, inside-jokey ways too. In the words of Anne Shirley of Green Gables, he was a kindred spirit, and by the end of the trip, he was a better friend and more attentive than John had ever been.

Standing at the bow, I watched as the boat brought us closer to shore. There was comfort in seeing land that I could swim to. I loved the sound of the water lapping against the boat, the feel of being small compared with the vastness of the sea and skies and stars. Light on water, whether it's the sun, moon, stars, neon signs, streetlights, or pool deck lights, thrills me, and it's almost easy to believe in water fairies flitting and dancing about on the waves. For three days, the old hymn "How Great Thou Art" had been my constant companion.

O Lord my God, When I in awesome wonder,
Consider all the worlds Thy hands have made:
I see the stars, I hear the rolling thunder,
Thy power throughout the universe displayed.

On dry ground, our group found our land legs, then grabbed a bite to eat (not fish) and started the seven-hour drive home. I'm not sure John and I uttered more than an occasional "I have to use the restroom" to each other. Alan was in the back seat, easing the tension between two people he'd begun to deeply care for, and who were on the brink of mutual resentment. Alan chatted with John, and he chatted with me, making us both laugh and giving us space not to take ourselves quite so seriously. (Two decades later, I'm still awed by Alan's ability to walk through territory filled with relational landmines.)

We arrived in Orlando and dropped Alan at home. My car was at John's house, so we ended our trip, and our relationship, there.

We unloaded John's car and he did most of the talking. Exactly what he said eludes me, but it probably went something like, "Leslie, you're a great girl but I think we'd be better off just being friends." I'd heard the sentiment before from the couple of guys I'd dated. It was tempting to believe I was the problem and that I was somehow, upon close inspection, simply unattractive. I finished putting my bags in my car and didn't say a thing except okay.

Then, on the drive home from John's house, I thought of all the things I wished I had said. So without hesitation, I turned around and drove back to his house. From the front window I could see he was already changed and watching football. I knocked and he grudgingly came to the door. He stood with one hand on the frame and the other on the doorknob, blocking me from coming inside the house.

"John," I said, pointing my finger close to his chest. He was nearly a foot taller than me. "John, you have something wrong with you." I was determined to be strong and say exactly what I thought. "You're a great guy. You have tons to offer a girl, but there's something wrong with you. You're closed off like something's missing or you're hiding something. You're going to need to figure it out if you're ever going to stay in a relationship. So figure it out." I see myself poking his chest on each of the last three words: *figure — it — out!*

As I turned and walked away from the house, I heard him close the door. I imagined him sitting down in his chair and watching the rest of the football game. He hadn't uttered a word. I got into my gold Volvo sedan, drove away, and cried all the way home. I knew I didn't love him. I knew we weren't meant to be together, but I was alone, again. I called Alan and told him all about it.

Several years and girlfriends later, John came out. You guessed it; he was gay. I suppose it's true what they say: mother knows best. Alan talked briefly with him about it all and he came to a few Exodus support groups, but we lost touch with him for years. Recently, at a memorial service for a good friend, we reunited. Afterward, we went to dinner at a restaurant, Dexter's, in downtown Orlando where I sat between John and Alan at a round table with our two children, and where Alan and I had sat many times before. Our friend who had passed away was one of my bridesmaids, and she had dated John after me. We remembered her and how she impacted our lives. We had a great time. John ordered grouper and I remembered he always liked fish. The three of us laughed as we talked about the fishing trip and how awkward it all was. We talked about God and how good he is. Hours later, John's boyfriend joined us. They've been together for almost fifteen years and met at the Exodus support group Alan led. Essentially, Alan can be credited with having introduced them. We laughed at the irony of it all and the kids got to meet one of Mommy and Daddy's oldest friends.

Shortly after the breakup with John, I was in Cleveland with the Hershisers, and only days away from my golden birthday; I was turning thirty on July 30. I was still single, and in the Christian community, where chastity before marriage is assumed, I was getting a little antsy. I was a nice person, wasn't I? Decent looking. I had an interesting job and good morals and I loved God. I imagined I was fun to be around since anyone could make me laugh. I was suitably independent. But I wanted a guy of my own.

There was no one on the horizon. I didn't feel I was being picky with my two-point list of what I wanted in a man. I had loved before and had been utterly rejected, and it was easy to slip into self-pity. Maybe I am ugly, or too strong, or, like poor Mrs. Mad Ox felt, I was simply too much. I wondered if the guys I'd met thought I was too much to handle. Or maybe they were just wimps. My emotions sat in a tree swing going back and forth, blaming myself, then others, for my loneliness.

In a more rational moment, I was able to get off the swing and remember that I had a good life. I lifted my head and hands in prayer and gave the fledgling gift of my future to God. My life had been in his capable hands for years and I knew it. I was simply reminding myself.

Later that day, as I was opening my mail in the kitchen, which included a few telltale handwritten envelopes that come on your birthday, I told Jamie and Orel all about breaking up with John, and my new friend Alan.

"Sooooo, this Alan. Is he more than a friend?" Jamie asked, optimistically.

"No. Not at all," I responded with absolute certainty. He was too much like Michael. Fun, for sure, but I just wasn't attracted to him. I've thought about it a lot, and I don't think it was because of the gay stuff. I really didn't think about that element of Alan's identity much at all. He was my friend, and whether he was gay, ex-gay, or hetero, it honestly didn't matter to me.

As I opened a manila envelope with my name on it, I found a VHS tape with a note from a friend that said, "Play me." Jamie and Orel and I exchanged glances, then I moved to the TV to play the mysterious tape.

On the tape, my group of friends, including Alan and not including John, sang a happy birthday song to me. Then Alan gave an impromptu rendition of "Somewhere over the Rainbow" in a show-stopping Ethel Merman style. He ended with a Broadway musical big finish body pose: eyes closed but to the sky, back slightly arched, and feet staggered. The Hershisers loved him instantly.

Back in Orlando, Alan and I were inseparable. We spent Sundays together and started skipping our Thursday night fellowship group, opting instead to stay at home with the Hershisers. Jamie cooked, Orel grilled, and occasionally I made an apple crisp. We watched *Friends*, *Seinfeld*, and *ER* and Alan became part of the family.

"What's your deepest, darkest secret?" Alan asked, sitting across from me at Dexter's, the restaurant in downtown Orlando. It was one of Alan's favorite lunch spots. He smiled and leaned in, his blue eyes full of intrigue and humor.

My eyes filled with tears and my face crumbled, making the formation of words impossible. "You don't have to tell me," he backtracked. "I just thought since you know all of my secrets, you wouldn't mind telling me yours." That wasn't fair. The world knew his secrets. He talked about them on TV.

I sat without uttering a word for almost an hour. We ate our salads or chicken or pasta, or whatever we'd ordered, in silence. I knew it was time to tell, but I didn't want to speak the words out loud.

"I had anonymous sex with men," he said lovingly. "How bad can your secret be?"

"Just listen and don't laugh," I said, moving the remaining bits and pieces of my meal around my plate with my fork. "There was no dog."

He laid his hand on top of mine begging me to turn my attention away from the dregs of my meal and to himself. "What do you mean, 'There was no dog'?"

"I mean there was no dog in my accident in April. There was *no* dog."

"Oh," was all he said with a hint of relief and laughter in his expression. I hadn't committed murder after all.

Six months earlier I was in a car accident, the one Alan had heard about at the hair salon.

My old Montero had finally died. Jamie knew my dream car was a forest green Jeep Cherokee, and she and Orel bought it for me. I was overcome with gratitude. It was forest green with tan leather interior, a year old, and it had been mine for three whole weeks before I'd totaled it.

I was on a road that curved around a lake near our house. I drifted onto the soft sandy shoulder, overcorrected, and the car flipped. Though it would be determined later that I was going only 32 mph, the car still managed to flip and spin several times before stopping in a lane of oncoming traffic. It was facing the opposite direction from which I had been traveling, passenger side to the ground, and I was suspended in air, hanging by my seat belt. Somehow, I unhooked my seat belt and crawled out of the hatch door. Someone helped me and kept me from further injuring myself on broken glass.

I sat on the side of the road and called Jamie, who was at the dentist. A police officer arrived while I was on the phone, and asked me what had happened. I didn't know what to say, but I did know I didn't want it to be my fault. Without thinking, I invented the story I would stick to for months. An ambulance took me to a hospital; the officer followed and questioned me again.

"I swerved to miss a dog," I said, lying on a table while the ER doctor removed broken glass and gravel from my left forearm.

"Hmm," he contemplated. "You know, you almost hit a jogger on the opposite side of the road. He says he never saw a dog." That's who must have helped me out of the car.

The doctor was stitching up my arm when the police officer left and met Jamie, who had just arrived. She and Orel owned the car and their insurance would foot the bill. A few minutes later, the officer left to file his report, and Jamie came to sit with me. "Hey, hon. Are you okay?"

"I'm okay," I said to the floor. "I'm so sorry."

The doctor finished stitching, gave us the name and number of a plastic surgeon we might want to visit, and then went about her duties with other patients who were worse off than me.

Helping me to get up and out of my curtained room, Jamie said, "The police officer wanted me to know he doesn't think there was a dog at the scene. He asked me what kind of employee you are and if I trusted you. He wanted to know if we were going to fire you." She caught my eyes. "I told him you were the best and I trusted you completely and of course you wouldn't be fired." I could barely look at her.

Jamie took care of me for a week while my arm was at its worst. She and Orel took care of all of the details with the totaled car. They argued with the insurance company that didn't want to insure me anymore and agreed to buy me a Volvo sedan—the safest car on the road. They never mentioned the dog or police officer again. They never held the financial details over my head, and they let me drive their children to school. Every time they were nice, it heaped more guilt on my head.

When Alan asked me about my deepest, darkest secret, I had one. My secret wasn't so much about what I'd done, though I was racked with guilt about it, but it was about who I had done it to. I'd lied to Jamie and Orel, and my parents, and to all of my friends. I hated that.

I trusted Alan, and confessing to him, through my tears, eased my shame and gave me the courage to take the next step. I confessed to Jamie as soon as I got home from lunch. As I walked into the room where she was contentedly flipping through a magazine, she looked up and said, "Hey, hon. How was lunch?" I told her my deepest darkest secret and that I intended to tell Orel too, knowing I might be fired.

She compassionately reiterated what she had said to the police officer and added, "Thank you for telling me. We love you. Orel comes home late tonight and I won't say anything to him. It's your story to tell."

I met Orel in the kitchen the next morning. Jamie took the boys to school and the house was quiet. "Do you have a minute?" I asked.

He casually leaned against the stove with his hands in his pockets and listened while I told my story. "We've always known there was no dog, Leslie. It didn't matter." He smiled sweetly and then he laid a wad of cash on the counter in front of me. "I was planning to give you this bonus simply because you've done such a good job with the boys. But now that you've told me, it makes giving it to you even more fun. We believe in you and want you to know how much we appreciate you. This is just a token." A token of grace.

I called Alan and told him all about it. With strength and compassion, he had led me into sharing the truth and leaving shame and guilt behind. He walked with me as I told my parents and friends. He joked with me even when it was too soon. I was learning to trust in and depend on him.

One November afternoon, Alan and I were eating lunch at Dexter's again, and it was becoming apparent that he cared for me in a way that I didn't reciprocate. It was getting uncomfortable.

And not because of his sexuality, which was something we simply almost never talked about. I believed that being gay was a part of Alan's past. He gave God the credit for changing him, and I knew God was big and entirely able to change a person, so I didn't really think much about it. So I didn't think of Alan in terms of gay or straight. He was just Alan. Maybe I was naive. Maybe because of who I am—my upbringing, my faith, my strengths and weaknesses, and my experiences all woven together—my ability to read people is strong, and I read Alan as someone who was honest and I had no reason to question him. Maybe it was both.

Twenty years later, I still don't think of Alan in terms of gay or straight. He is just my Alan. My husband. For a time, if pressed, I would have called him ex-gay, but that term always seemed to get caught in my throat. There's freedom in not having to define him based on who he is or isn't attracted to—other than, of course, the binding tie of "Yours" at the end of every note he's ever left me. There's freedom in loving him as he is and not wanting to change him. There's freedom in understanding that it's not my job to change anyone, for that matter, let alone to declare that a gay person should change. God's love transcends sexual orientation. God's love transcends everything. My purpose in life—in our marriage, with our children and our neighbors—is to love. Radically, fully, beyond measure, without hindrance. Maybe, somehow, twenty years ago, I was a work in progress, beginning to understand there's freedom in following Jesus' example and living life with no other agenda than declaring who his good Father is and loving people.

So Alan liked me. A lot. It had become obvious from the way he looked at me, followed me, called me, sat with me for hours as I ironed, and made sure I was having fun and was cared for. I knew that he liked me as more than just a good friend.

When lunch was over, he suggested we walk around nearby Lake Eola. I somehow knew what was coming, even though I had never been on this side of the relationship coin.

"You know I like you, right?" Alan finally said as

we walked along the lakeshore. Swans swam. Children played. A man walked by with his Chihuahua, the four-pound dog leading the way, stretching the auto-release leash to maximum length.

By "like" I knew he meant as more than a friend. He was my best friend; how could I *not* know? "I know," I said. Wanting to be clear and to protect my friend, I continued, "There was a boy I liked, and when I told him, he said he didn't want to hurt me and proceeded to tell me everything he liked about me all the while stringing me on. I like you too much and won't do that to you. I have to be honest. It's never going to happen, Alan."

"Okay," he said to my surprise, smiling, reassuring me we'd still be friends. "Can you believe that guy with the dog? Wonder who wears the pants in his family." Alan laughed and mercifully changed the subject.

Alan then backed off. Which was fine for a while, because life was busy and it seemed okay. But then, at a New Year's Eve party, he ignored me, and I was annoyed. Being an introvert, I have an aversion to socializing on my own at big events with lots of people. He was supposed to be my anchor. But hours later, he asked me to dance. And although I didn't realize it at the time, I felt much better.

Alan turned twenty-five in February 1997. When I arrived to his party, he made room for me next to him at dinner. Afterward, he walked me to my car and hugged me goodnight. I remember a funny little feeling, a gentle squeeze in my heart, and I noticed how well we physically fit together. I drove home savoring the hug and questioning my feelings, and wondering if I'd eaten something that disagreed with me. It couldn't be that I liked him. The next two days were my days off, and I stayed in my room, which seemed to spin with questions. What was that feeling? Did I like him? Was that feeling real? Did I imagine it? How can I like him? He's just Alan.

By the third day, I was beginning to think differently. "What *if* I like him?" I looked at a picture with Alan on my left and two other friends on my right. I covered up the two on the right just to see what we looked like together. I smiled. *We* looked nice. I shook my head and hid the photograph under my bed as if putting the picture under my bed would make the questions go away.

Moments later, I pulled the picture out again, and placed my hand over my friends' faces, this time for a bit longer. I felt confused. I knew how he felt about me, and I was realizing how I felt about him. For months, he had looked at me like Mr. Darcy looked at Elizabeth Bennett, like Mr. Rochester looked at Jane Eyre, like Gilbert Blythe looked at Anne Shirley, like Captain von Trapp looked at Maria. And like all of these women, I was slowly realizing how much that affection meant to me. He met my two "what I want in a husband" list items, and now, I was attracted to him. It was all coming together.

Alan liked me first and had subtly pursued me for months. No guy, except John, for a total of about two seconds, had ever done that. Alan had an inner strength, a confidence without improper pride (thank you again, Elizabeth Bennett), a depth and love for God I'd never seen before. Alan had proven himself trustworthy, someone with whom I could share my secrets. I could follow him—walk with him—anywhere. *This is it*, I suddenly thought. And I knew. I was in love.

Never say never—there's a reason the adage holds its own. My desire to be pursued and my "it's never going to happen" left me in a bit of a pickle, so I set out to drop a few subtle clues. I simply smiled and said okay when he told me he was thinking about taking a job at the Exodus International office in Seattle and jokingly told me I should go with him. And I comfortably put my hand on his knee and left it there throughout a dinner with friends. And I took his arm and pulled myself close to his side as we sauntered down his beloved Park Avenue, and within a week, he asked me out.

It was Monday, March 10, and Alan asked if I wanted to go to dinner, a totally normal thing for us, which, in this case, was definitely *not* normal. We both knew that this was more than dinner. When he picked me up that evening, I was in my room and ready, in every sense of the word, but needed a second to breathe and pray for this relationship to be God's kind of good, a phrase I often prayed when I wasn't sure whether to trust my own sense of what was right. I was nervous, not because of *who* it was but rather because of *what* it was. Jamie, Orel, both boys, and Alan hung in the kitchen laughing and waiting for me.

In a movie scene, I would have walked down a long, curving stairway. Alan would meet me at the foot of the stairs and take my hand as I stepped off the final step and toward him. But instead, I walked a few flat feet into the kitchen. There was no horse-drawn carriage, only Alan's white Honda and the Hershisers standing on the porch waving us off like they were the Beverly Hillbillies. There was a single red rose and two Hallmark cards, both expressing his love for me, in the passenger seat. We held hands on the long drive to the Wilderness Lodge on Disney property. Halfway through the meal, sitting across from me, he smiled, leaned in, his blue eyes blazing with intrigue and humor, and said, "So when are we getting married?"

My response was cool and quick. "January third is a Saturday."

He drove me home, and on the front steps in front of the house took my face in his hands and kissed me (in my favorite of all comparisons) like Mr. Thornton kissed Margaret at the end of the BBC version of Elizabeth Gaskell's *North and South*. From the beginning, he led the way in our relationship: emotionally and physically.

Before the sun rose on January 3, 1998, I stood in the bathroom getting ready for my big day. *Here we go*, I thought. I was well rested and filled with a knowing peace. I wasn't worried about the day or the much-anticipated wedding night; I was a thirty-one-year-old virgin—not quite a movie title, I suppose, but a reality nonetheless—but of course, I was nervous. In truth, Alan was so public about his sexuality, we had rarely talked about his orientation and how it would affect us. We went to a couple of pre-marital classes at a church, which addressed issues like finances and family traditions, but never sexuality. The only conversation we really had about sex was when Alan mentioned that maybe we should wait until we were in Jamaica on our honeymoon. We were to spend our first night together in Orlando after a long day of wedding festivities. He mentioned a friend of his suggested waiting, and I understood we would both be exhausted. I was a little disappointed, but I figured I'd waited this long, what was one more night?

Putting on my mascara, I confidently breathed what had been my daily prayer for the last time. "Lord, I've grown more sure every day we've dated that this relationship with Alan is good, but I've been wrong before, and I need you. I'm asking you to stop this thing if it's not your kind of good." I added with a smile, "We're pretty far down this road and I realize if you're going to stop it today, it's going to have to be in a big way—another car accident or something—but I'd rather you do that than me miss your direction, so have at it. Thanks."

But I arrived at the church unscathed. Alan and I both said "I do" in the company of family and friends who knew our stories, and together we embarked on a road full of twisting curves and beautiful scenery. And I believe with all my heart that it has indeed been God's kind of good. Which is the best kind of good there is.

CHAPTER 8

THE NIGHT

"It's okay. We're okay," Leslie said, her bare body holding onto mine as I sobbed. Her voice, like her body, was strong and soft and comforting. It was our second night in Jamaica, our third as Mr. and Mrs. Alan Chambers. It was *the* night. The one in which we'd planned to consummate our marriage. But things didn't go as planned.

I have to pause here and admit that this chapter is tricky.

Leslie and I are writing together, sitting across from one another on two matching white couches in our Florida sunroom, which is encased by a long wall of windows that fills the room with natural light. The windows frame our back yard, where years ago we planted a perimeter of viburnum that is now over six feet tall and three feet thick. It's a beautiful hedge of protection that keeps a private space for our family. Leslie has just such a hedge around the space that is intimately ours alone: our sex life. But that's not what makes writing this chapter tricky.

There are those who think our marriage is a farce.

Leslie received this message just a few days ago on her Facebook account: "Your marriage is a SHAM, you have fetishized your husband's sexuality and allowed him to fetishize you in a disgusting and unnatural way. ... Your marriage is disgusting. ... There is no forgiveness for MONSTERS like you, just the burning desire that you vanish. ... Shame on you. Divorce. Make amends to your children, and get a life."

For her, messages like that are worth about as much consideration as the ones she's received touting she's a saint for marrying a man like me and staying with me even though I have "issues." But prejudices like these do not make telling our story tricky either.

It gets tricky when, motivated by a desire to be honest and vulnerable, we set out to write about our lives together and think about our kids reading this chapter someday. Or our moms. Ahead is our truth and vulnerability, wrapped in a hedge of protection that hopefully won't send our kids into therapy or our mothers to their cardiologists.

Frankly, none of this is anyone's business anyway. After all, there are some things that are meant to remain between a husband and his wife. But it's also a fundamental part of the story we're telling, so here goes. Kids, Mom: you might want to skip this one.

Our wedding had been beautiful. We were married at First Baptist Winter Park, where as a child I dreamed of such a wedding day from my seat in the balcony. The church teemed with garland, wreaths, and bows from Christmas, and at a sunny 73 degrees, even the weather was perfect. The ceremony began at 10:30 a.m., and we had most of our pictures taken beforehand. We had two receptions, a sit-down brunch at a country club immediately after the ceremony for our two hundred guests, and an intimate dinner party that evening at the Hershisers' reserved just for our immediate families and the wedding party—about fifty people.

Before a radiant Leslie walked down the aisle to "Trumpet Voluntary," I escorted my mom and dad to their seats. Tears of contentment fell as I walked the same aisle toward the altar where so many years ago I met and fell in love with Jesus and where I had prayed so many times for God to make me straight. Tears of gratitude fell knowing I was reconciled with my dad and that he was proud of me and loved Leslie. Tears of joy fell knowing I was marrying the very person I was created to spend my life with. With my friends and family surrounding me, all of whom knew my story, it was one of the single greatest moments of my life.

It's so important for me to say that I wasn't marrying Leslie with any unresolved anxiety about my sexuality or secretly longing for a different life. Despite my lifelong attraction to men, still resident within, I was completely and wholeheartedly in love with and attracted to Leslie. Leslie was my first choice and never a backup plan. She wasn't my consolation prize for not acting on my gay feelings. She was who and what I wanted most. When Leslie's dad gave me her hand, which I had called and asked him for months prior, I knew without a shadow of a doubt it would be until death. But a gauntlet lay ahead.

Many of my nonmarried Exodus friends found the idea of sex with a woman repulsive. I never felt that way. I had crushes on many girls and dated and kissed a fair number of them. My encounters with men had been without pleasantries or relationships or even names for that matter, and were few and far between. And even in those instances, I struggled with performance despite my attractions and desire.

I made a point to talk about honeymoon sex with married Exodus and non-Exodus friends before Leslie and I got married. Two of them said, "Take the pressure off yourselves. You and Leslie are going to be tired the first night. Determine ahead of time to just fool around and get to know one another. Save sex for a night when you're fully rested." One recommended waiting until the third night. I clung to that formula. Having sex with anyone was a scary prospect. It was an act of vulnerability and, in my mind, required a perfect performance. Anne Lamott in *Bird by Bird* says, "Perfection is the voice of the oppressor, the enemy of the people." It's so true. As a lifelong approval addict, failure and looking—even more than being—out of control plagues me.

"In the past," I said to Leslie, sitting next to her in a booth at a crowded restaurant about six months before our wedding, "when I've had sex with a man, it's been all about me." It was an honest conversation, probably better suited for a secluded spot, but I really wanted to talk with her about the third-day idea I had learned from my friend. "I didn't know or want to know the other guy," I continued. "I simply wanted to accomplish my task and get out of there. I don't want sex to be like that with you. I don't want sex like that ever again. I'd like to take things slowly—maybe wait until we're in Jamaica. What do you think?"

I remember Leslie being completely present in that conversation. None of this fazed her. This was just the couple we were becoming. Who we would always be. She moved me with her steadfastness. She and I had extraordinarily different pasts, and yet we had an ability to have conversations that transcended our histories. We understood each other.

And Leslie understood waiting until the second night, but was a little disappointed at the prospect of waiting until the third. We agreed to see how things played out.

I loved the third-day advice because I wanted everything to be just perfect and not rushed or forced, but I also got some advice I didn't value as much—at least not at first. I was in love with Leslie and loved sharing about my engagement with people who knew my story. So when I ran into my friend Margaret at a restaurant one afternoon while I was hanging out with Victor, I expected her to be thrilled. She was a fifty-something widow whom I considered to be as fabulous as a drag queen. I hadn't seen her in months, and I was craving a dose of her fabulousness. But her response surprised me.

"You know, Alan," she said, more serious than exuberant, "sex does not equal intimacy." She peered down at me like she had X-ray vision into my very soul.

"I. Know." I said it with a forced smile. What I wanted to say was, "Thanks for nothing, Captain Obvious."

"Sex does not equal intimacy," she repeated, then returned to her lunch date.

Between the two wedding receptions, we checked into our hotel room and had a few hours to relax. As soon as the door shut behind the bellman, we were alone in our first place together as a married couple, and there was no hesitation to hop into the shower together. No inhibition. Being with Leslie was natural and comfortable. I had struggled for years with body image insecurities, but with her they were nonexistent. It's like Leslie and I had started our life together before we'd even met, and it's easy to see her in my story even before I knew she existed. Being with her, with nothing between us, felt like something we'd done forever. I couldn't keep my hands off her milky white skin, adorned with freckles. She had been a competitive swimmer, and being fit was important to her. While on the fishing trip where we became friends, I remember how she looked in her black one-piece swimsuit with white piping. She had strong arms and shoulders, perfect breasts, and a flat stomach, all leading to the most beautiful curvature where her muscular legs began. She dove like a pro into the Atlantic

Ocean. In the two years I'd known her, I had memorized her every visible feature. In the ten months of our engagement, I had dreamed of the rest.

"I don't think I'm going to have any problem with sex," I gushed to one of my groomsmen a couple of hours later while sipping champagne and eating canapes at the party. "Leslie and I fooled around at the hotel, and it was fun and everything worked like it should. We could have had sex right there. I'm so happy. What was I so worried about?"

By the time we got back to the hotel, we were exhausted and decided to stick to our day-three plan, and all we got was a good night's sleep.

The next day was almost as full as the previous, but ended up being more stressful. We started with breakfast in bed, thoroughly enjoying just being together. We took care of details like giving Leslie's wedding dress and my tux to a friend and checked in for our flight, which was scheduled for later that day.

Finally, after several annoying flight delays, we landed in Jamaica and stood at the baggage carousel waiting for our luggage. Fellow passengers grabbed their bags and started their vacations. Finally, a lone black suitcase with an orange ribbon tied to its handle circled the carousel and whispered to us at every lap, "I'm still not yours." Empty-handed, we approached a small bus promising to carry us safely to our destination, a resort in Ocho Rios. Actually, there was no promise, just our hope.

It was dark. We took our seats on a crowded little bus

mixed with locals and tourists. The bus left the vicinity of the airport, and I held on to Leslie as each pothole on the narrow road threatened to toss us out the open windows or onto the floor. I expected a short shuttle ride to the hotel, but we drove for well over an hour. We could hear crickets singing and a cat or bird or some unknown primate screech. I imagined being murdered by headhunters or cannibals like the ones on *Gilligan's Island*. I was Mowgli before Bagheera saved him from Shere Kahn in *The Jungle Book*. As the nauseating smell of warm overdressed flesh hovered just below my nostrils, I longed for the simple comforts of home, like air-conditioning and personal space bubbles. Leslie is a trooper and did her best to take my mind off of it all, but I think even she was beginning to wonder whether we'd reach our destination. Eventually, we made a sharp left through some impressive iron gates and into a beautifully tropical open-air hotel. It was kind of like *Fantasy Island*, and I looked for Tattoo.

We checked in, informed the front desk attendant about our luggage, which the airline representative assured us was forthcoming, and went to our room. Having endured all I could for one day, I showered and got into bed. Had there been a minibar in our room, I'd have emptied it. Thus ended our second day of our marriage. It was easy to stick to the day-three plan that night, and we got another good night's sleep.

Day three was packed with nothing to do and therefore was nearly as stressful as the previous two. I privately felt the gauntlet of our approaching night draw nearer.

Thankfully, our luggage arrived, and afterward, we laid out in the sun and then ate dinner. We explored the hotel, and eventually each other. From the moment she had walked into our room that night, my heart pounded, and Leslie was my only desire. But soon enough, perhaps out of nervousness or feelings of pressure, I wasn't able to turn our fooling around into intercourse, and heartbreak set in. Dejected and miserable, I wondered if I had ruined Leslie's life by asking her to marry less than a real man.

Lying in a heap in the messy-from-fooling-around bed overlooking the Caribbean Sea, I remembered Margaret's then-strange and now-eerily-appropriate admonishment. "Sex does not equal intimacy," she'd said, presumptively. But I was now struck by how laser-pointed the wisdom was, and how badly I needed it in that moment.

After several quiet and disappointed moments between us, Leslie turned to me and uttered the most selfless words I'd ever heard. She took my breath away. "We had fun tonight. Everything worked perfectly up until that last part, and I didn't marry you for the sex. I married you because I love you and we have a lifetime to figure all of this out. We will figure it out, I have no doubt. Even if I had known tonight would end like this, I still would've married you."

I looked at her, tears in my eyes, wordless but full of love.

"It's okay. We're okay," she said.

Each Jamaican moment that passed, I better understood Leslie as God's greatest earthly gift to me. We had a blast together poolside in the sun and gasping in horror at the gaunt eighty-something-year-old woman who insisted on lying at a 90 degree angle, upside down in her chaise lounge, topless. We drank pina coladas, ate, climbed Dunn River Falls, walked on the beach, shopped, smelled the sweet unmistakable scent of unseen individuals smoking marijuana, and spent every evening intimately finding out new things about each other and ourselves.

"We're writing our story," Leslie said on the final night of our honeymoon, when we had yet to fully experience *the* night. Dressed in our island finest, sitting in the dimly lit restaurant looking more deeply into each other's eyes than either of us had ever experienced, we held hands, continuing our unique and very happily ever after. "It's challenging now, and we don't understand it, but we will tell this story someday." The stress melted away.

———— ∞ ————

Eight months and twenty-three days post wedding day, with surprise and unmeasured relief, Leslie and I consummated our marriage. Officially. After our honeymoon, we briefly consulted a counselor, who encouraged us to relax and take our time. Leslie and I shared our struggles with a few friends, one of whom, with no history of same-sex attraction, told us it had taken them six weeks to figure it out. I remembered hearing of another couple who hadn't had sex in ten years. Everything else in our marriage was great. Intimacy had grown, even without technically having sex, and was flourishing.

In hindsight, Leslie and I realized that one of the major obstacles to our problems was tragically and yet comically simple: we simply didn't know to go to our local drugstore and buy a bottle of K-Y. And soon, my anxiety over being inadequate became the more significant barrier. But honestly, in the end, I don't exactly know why it was so hard for us. But I do know that I became so used to feeling defective that I was sure every problem we encountered was my fault. Still, in the eight months and twenty-three days prior to official consummation, we were otherwise intimate on a nightly basis. I studied Leslie's body and she studied mine. We might not have had "official sex," but neither of us was left wanting.

When our first time together was over, we cried again and had a slightly awkward, but real, "thank-you Jesus" moment. We wondered how people, kids even, who didn't love each other felt after such moments. We had worked rather hard for it, actually. We'd been patient and learned about each other and wondered at the rarity that was ours. Neither of us had ever experienced anything of the sort, but we would again. And again. And again.

It's been seventeen years since that first January third. My job and my lack of a job and a dog who is afraid of fireworks and a cat who jumped on the bed and kids who jump in the bed and one of the four posts on our bed falling and hitting me square on my bare back and hurricanes and a short season of trying to control my ADHD with Wellbutrin have all inhibited us on occasion, but we've learned to laugh at such things. Intimacy, love, friendship, commonality, union, grace, and, yes, sex have grown unhindered.

Sex is not the qualifier for our existence as a happily married couple, but if it were, we'd be good. I've heard it said that as a married couple, if you put a penny in a box every time you had sex the first year of marriage and then took one out every time you had sex after the first year, you'd never run out of pennies. For us, that simply hasn't been true.

So have my same-sex attractions interfered with our marriage, you ask? My unequivocal answer is this: not any more than Leslie's opposite-sex attraction to Richard Armitage.

CHAPTER 9

MY TRUE SELF

My story is my own, a truth I didn't get until recent years. For all intents and purposes, I am a man who was born gay. For the sake of the point I'm trying to make, let's define gay merely as homosexual. I realize the word is outdated, but hang with me. Homosexual is (simply) defined as a person who is sexually attracted to the same sex. I didn't come out of the womb longing for sex with other boys, of course, but wrapped up in that light blue baby blanket, all warm and soft and cuddly, were all of the makings of a gay man.

As I matured, those ingredients burgeoned and in the great big Kitchen Aid of my life, mixed with early childhood experiences, perceptions, and biology in time resulted in a gay—same-sex attracted—teenager and man. If my life had been different, would I have still been gay? I don't know, probably. But that's not the point, and frankly all the pontificating is a distraction. "I was born gay" is important because there is very little I, or anyone else for that matter, can do about who they are attracted to—heteros, homos, bad boys, tall girls, you name it.

But wait—there's more.

I am also a man who is joyfully married to a woman. To Leslie. We have two beautiful children. We're a family—that basic, fundamental unit of life—which is an experience that has been known by all cultures throughout all time. Leslie is now and has been my very first choice, the only person I have loved and been intimate and sexually active with over the course of twenty years.

To wear any one label would explain only a fraction of who I am. I cannot deny any part of the truth of my story—be it attractions, experiences, or beliefs. But until recently, I haven't been able to confidently own all of these things equally in every setting. The level of gratitude I feel for the grace to humbly and openly experience my identity is something I cannot adequately express in words.

"Your story is nice and all, but your cute little stereotypes of what it means to be gay and your experience is [screwed] up." Katie, an editor from the *Washington Blade*, was seething. She was brought on the show, from what I understood, to refute my story of changing from gay to straight. "I'm sorry, but you were never really gay." She looked too much like Sinead O'Connor for it to be an accident, and from the moment Ricki Lake introduced her, sitting in the second row, she seemed ready to do battle with me. She appeared on edge, like she was wounded, cornered in a back alley by some unknown beast that meant to do her harm. She caught sight of the cameraman. "Sorry for the swear word."

The show's premise was gay men dating women. The women came on the show expecting a proposal or a deepening commitment from their boyfriends but were to be told by the men that there wasn't any hope for a future because they were gay. The title was "Baby, I'm Gay" or something like that. Leslie and I had been happily married for a little over ten months when Ricki's producers, who found me through Exodus, called. Though it all seemed a bit dodgy, we were motivated by the chance to share *our* story and the opportunity for an impromptu and all-expenses-paid trip to New York City.

The *Ricki Lake* studio audience was filled with a curious mix of people. LGBT folks like Katie, and a group of women from a local black church that cheered me on as if I were their pastor preaching to the choir. "That's right," said a fabulous black woman in response to nearly everything that came out of my mouth. Her pillbox hat was a major focus for me during my first experience on national television.

"Alan says he's gone from gay to straight," Ricki said, insinuating her bias, as Leslie joined me onstage. "His wife Leslie is proof." Then Ricki addressed Leslie. "Come on, Leslie. Alan has admitted he's gay. You've got to be constantly wondering, 'What if he cheats on me?'" Ricki said, almost begging my wife to see the error of her ways and come clean in front of millions of viewers. Ricki looked to the audience for support and coaxed them to give an emotional response. "What will you do when it happens?"

Leslie quickly responded, "What would you do if your husband cheated on you, Ricki? If it happens, I—"

"I'll divorce him!" Ricki interrupted, quickly garnering the sought-after reaction of a roaring audience.

Leslie pressed on, "I'm not worried about it. If I thought he would cheat on me, I wouldn't have married him in the first place. But if it happens, we'll work through it. I won't waste any time wondering or worrying about it. I love him. I trust him. And that's enough." The crowd quieted and Ricki moved on to other more audacious guests.

We'd arrived at the studio in a limo about four hours before the taping and were immediately separated. Leslie was taken to a holding room with the women who would be on the show, and I was with the men. I quickly learned that Leslie and I were very different from our castmates. We weren't going onstage to drop or receive any bomblike information.

In the men's greenroom, the guys started to chat with each other. "Why are you here?" was a question we all asked and eventually answered. Tony, a handsome tattooed and pierced twenty-two-year-old, was there to tell his baby mama he just wanted to be gay. Another guy whose name I cannot recall was supposed to have a story like mine. His mannerisms were twitchy and bordered on outrageous, and unfortunately the audience seemed to laugh at, and not with, him. He was there with his wife too. For the taping, she wore nondescript baggy clothes that hid her frame and a wig that made her look like Velma from *Scooby Doo*. She changed her name so her coworkers wouldn't know her.

Robby, a nice boy from Texas, was there to tell his dearest friend he wasn't in love with her and never would be. "I know Heather is expecting me to pledge my love to her today. She's going to be devastated when I tell her I'm not attracted to her at all and that I'm gay." Robby was tied up in knots and freaking out. His cheeks were beet red and he kept pulling on the neck of his crewneck wool sweater trying to cool off. "Alan, what do you think I should say? I don't want to hurt her."

"Be honest, but if you say, 'I'm not attracted to you *at all*,' she'll feel devastated and unattractive. Why not say, 'Heather, I love you. You're my very best friend. You're beautiful and smart and funny. We have the best time together. But I'm gay. I want you to fall in love with someone who will love you back in the way you deserve to be loved'?"

When Robby went onstage, he used my words verbatim.

Whether the show had any lasting value, I'm not sure. At the end of the day, the boys were planning to go to a gay bar, and I'm not sure whether the girls joined them. I heard Katie was fired by her boss because of her on-air antics. Sadly, a few years later Ricki did divorce her husband. And I was publicly linked as an official Exodus spokesperson for the first time, which invited critique from a community who saw me simply as the latest addition to a long line of oppressors. It took me a very, very long time to fully grasp this fact.

———— ∞∞∞ ————

From the moment we started dating, Leslie and I looked for opportunities to tell her parents about me. My parents and siblings, my church, and anyone who listened to Christian radio or watched Christian television in Central Florida knew my ex-gay story, which, in my narcissism, felt like the whole world. But Leslie's family lived in California. There was no internet access or Facebook for them to do a quasi background check, but the truth would eventually get to them. Ex-gay was a label I wore because nothing else seemed to fit. It highlighted the fact that there had been some degree of gay at one time, and for most Christians, any amount of gay was enough to give Jesus, Mary, and Joseph a coronary. We expected it to be a difficult conversation to have over the phone and before they met me, so we decided to wait until we could talk face to face.

We made two trips to Fresno before our wedding, and in all the time we were alone with them, there was not one good moment—not one, I swear—to tell them about me. Our days were packed visiting other family members and friends. The first time Leslie had alone with her mom was one week before the wedding. It seems preposterous, but it's true.

Her mom flew to Orlando the day after Christmas, and her dad and other family members were to arrive a couple of days later. That night in the guest room where her mom was staying, they sat on the bed and talked.

"Mom," Leslie said, "I have something I want to talk to you about. Don't freak out. Just listen." Which is enough to freak any mother out. She told her everything.

The next day, as the three of us drove to my parents' house for dinner in Leslie's gold Volvo sedan, I looked in the rearview mirror. "Do you have any questions for me, Sue?" We'd been driving for twenty minutes and had about thirty more to go. I knew Leslie had finally shared my story, now our story, with her mom. An elephant in a small car is even more of a painful nuisance than one in a living room. I was ready for anything to be said, just to ease the tension.

She gently cleared her throat. "I just want to know that you're going to be faithful to my daughter. I want you to promise me that. I want to know that you've promised her that." Her voice was direct in her admonishment with only a hint of uncertainty as she addressed her soon to be (ex-gay) son-in-law.

At a stoplight, I turned around and looked her in the eye and said, "Sue, I promise you I will be faithful to God. I can't promise perfection. No one can. But I love Leslie. I want Leslie. Because I love God, I will be faithful to him, and in that I will be faithful to Leslie. That's all any of us can promise."

We arrived at my parents' home and Sue saw me interact with my family. She spent time with the Hershisers who had been eyewitnesses to and encouraged our developing relationship. On the night I proposed to Leslie, Jamie, Orel, and the boys had TP'd Leslie's room and waited up to see the engagement ring. Most of all, Sue watched her daughter and me together. She watched and trusted God and Leslie and me.

———— ∞ ————

People on all sides of the great debate, like Katie, have demanded that I declare myself, that I give myself a label. Either I never was gay or I am still gay or I'm ex-gay or bisexual. One group wants me to own my gayness and admit I'm in a mixed orientation marriage. Another wants me to own my gayness and leave my family. Another would rather I not talk about said gayness but deny my feelings and "claim victory" over them. And still another desperately wants me to proclaim I'm now straight and change is possible. I've lost friends because I won't wear their chosen label. I have long said none of these labels fully describe me. While I resist the gay label, straight isn't going to be a trophy I put on my shelf either.

There are a few labels I can give myself without complication or explanation. I am, in fact, a man. I am a son. A brother. A husband. A father. A Christian. Those things are indisputable.

As a believer in Jesus, I am not Baptist or Anabaptist or Arminian or Calvinist or anything—I am just a simpleminded Jesus lover. As a human, I am sexual. I have found in life that no sexual experience, whether with a man or all alone, feels better than it does with Leslie. Sex with Leslie is full of memories, stories, travels in far-off countries like Iceland and Ecuador and Greece and many spots in between, that first time in our first apartment, many times on visits home in the room where she grew up, late nights on the family room floor in our first house, in our beloved New York City on a cold morning in our hotel room when we had to be deathly quiet so as not to wake our small children, who were sound asleep in the bed next to us. No sexual experience has ever been as satisfying as sex with Leslie. Leslie is the love of my life. And that's why I determined to share this part of life with her and only her *from this day forward* all those years ago.

I once heard a pastor who happens to be over six feet tall say that he is attracted to tall women. He said it's likely his sexual orientation. He went on to say that he has been happily married to his four-foot-eleven wife for more than forty years without incident. It's not a perfect analogy, but it has parallels for sure.

I don't mind people labeling themselves or me as gay. I completely understand how much easier it is to just say, "I'm gay." It's a statement that reflects certain facts. I am attracted to men. I notice them. The thought of sex with a man is not abnormal or gross to me. That aspect of my orientation never changed. Not even a little. So to label myself straight would be an outright lie.

———— ∞∞∞ ————

During many speaking engagements and media interviews as the president of Exodus International, I talked about a diminishing of my same-sex attractions or how they had changed drastically. I think part of this was wrapped up in how I felt about Leslie. I understood that truly gay men wouldn't feel about a woman the way I felt about Leslie, so that must have meant I'd changed or was changing. Through the years, I've come to see things more clearly. Attractions are different from temptations.

Like I said, my same-sex attractions hadn't changed. But my sexual temptations did. They *did* diminish. What actually changed for me was the insatiable need I once had for sex with a man. It's not like I'm constantly holding myself back from jumping in bed with a man. What truly stops me is the same thing that would stop me if my orientation was primarily toward women: faithfulness to God first and my wife second. Sex *doesn't* equal intimacy. The allure of the forbidden is tempting no matter what you are tempted toward. An orgasm with a man would last about five minutes and would seriously alter a life I dearly love and value above all else. It's not worth it. I don't want it. I want what I already have.

During one interview with a national newspaper, a gay reporter concluded his interview with me and asked if we could talk off the record for a few minutes. This was often how interviews went for me. "Don't you feel like you are denying your true self, Alan?" the journalist queried kindly.

"Let me answer it this way," I said. "It's Friday. When I am finished with this interview, I will drive home. At home, I will put on a baggy T-shirt, a pair of expandable waist shorts, and huge-framed glasses, and order a pepperoni pizza from Giovanni's and probably watch *Mary Poppins* with my wife and kids. That's my true self, my true life, and I *love* it."

I want to spend the rest of my life with Leslie. My love for her on the day I proposed—on our first date—was reason enough to ask. But it has grown exponentially every day since. I love investing in our life together. I love that we have a hundred gazillion stories together, have looks that only we can fully decipher, and are the only people neither of us ever grow weary of. She is the only person I truly want in every single way. I do not desire to know anyone and to be known by anyone in the way I know Leslie and am known by her. Those of you who have found what I am talking about—whether you are with a same-sex partner or opposite—understand this point.

So who am I? I'm a son of God, a husband, a father, a son, a son-in-law, a brother, a brother-in-law, an uncle, a cousin, and a friend. I'm Alan. And what's my orientation? Leslie. My orientation is Leslie.

CHAPTER 10

LIKE FATHER, LIKE SON

As I looked out the window, the hum of the jet engine was lulling me into a daze and my mind replayed scenes from the previous two months. It was 2007 and I was headed to Southern California for the Thirty-Second Annual Exodus Freedom Conference.

Like every year of my presidency at Exodus, I would be the keynote speaker on opening night, and my preparation for these addresses required hours of deep personal introspection. This year would be an emotional one. A building upon of the things I'd shared at the conference a year prior, the one just on the heels of my fateful conversation with my employee Matt, the one in which he changed my life by telling me he'd never be like me and I responded by telling him I wasn't straight.

Isaac was in the seat between the window and me. Leslie and Molly in the two seats across the aisle. It was our first time on a plane in those two months. As I looked out the window, I thought about the last time we'd all flown together, after receiving a much-anticipated call regarding my dad.

"Al, 's Dad." He was a master at running words together in the most endearing and somehow educated of ways. "I want to talk to you about somethin'." It was like the evening he announced he was going back to church. Now, twenty years later, with that same east Tennessee parlance, Dad had another announcement.

"Son, I want you to listen. Don't say anything until I am done talkin'. I don't want to interrupt your trip."

Those words sent me into travel-planning mode. Leslie, the kids, and I were in Fresno on a much-needed vacation at my in-laws'. We'd gotten there only the day before. Fresno in April is near perfection as far as weather goes. I had been preparing for my first nap in months when my cell phone vibrated and I saw "Mom & Dad" on the caller ID.

Diagnosed with type II diabetes in 1970, my dad's body had finally given out, and his will to live had followed suit. Though he'd tried time and again during my lifetime, he never successfully got a good handle on his love for food. He was a chef and restaurateur and a true southern boy to boot. He and Paula Deen could have hung out. They would have bonded like pimento cheese on a Ritz. Diabetes had ravaged his body and led to heart disease, vascular disease, kidney failure, legal blindness, and the amputation of both legs below the knee. He was ready to see Jesus.

"I want you and Lez and the kids to enjoy your time in Fresno with Bob and Sue. I just want you to know I love you and I'm tired of hurtin'. I'm tired of hospitals, and I'm goin' home."

He was calling from his room at Winter Park Hospital. It was where so many of my nieces and nephews had been born, where my sister Patti surrendered her appendix in 1982, and where I'd had surgery to repair a broken arm on Father's Day 1985. Most important, it is where I first met my own adopted son, then named Baby Boy Doe, less than twenty-four hours after he'd been born and dropped off by someone who said they couldn't take care of him but wanted him to be safe.

Winter Park Hospital was a place Dad had frequented over the last two decades, starting with his first heart attack in 1989—the night Lucille Ball died. This time he was there because of excruciating back pain. After eight years of dialysis, his bones were crumbling inside his body. He'd had enough.

"I'm not doing any more dialysis, and I'm going to go home with Mom." He'd finally made the unfathomable choice the doctors had once explained was inevitable.

My dad knew me so well. Our relationship was unrecognizable from the one we shared thirteen years and eight months prior. It had astonished me when I realized we were cut from the same cloth. He knew there was no way I was going to do anything but get on a plane with my family and come home. He knew I was going to burst into tears any minute and try to pretend I wasn't crying. He knew, and he was right.

I hung up and walked through the back door across the small porch nestled under flowering vine-covered arbors and into the lush back yard. Isaac and Molly were playing with their cousins. As my bare feet pressed into soft angel-hair grass, I repeated the conversation I'd had with my dad to Leslie.

A gentle "oh honey" from Leslie and I burst into tears. And so did she. I fell into her strong and capable embrace. Between sobs and stuttered breathing, I imagined a life without the dearest, most complicated man I knew.

After the first wave of shock and grief was over, I had to find a way to get us home. I wouldn't go on this journey without my family. The kids needed to see Pa Pa, and he needed to see them. My dad adored Leslie possibly as much as he did me, and Isaac and Molly were two of his most prized possessions. We just all needed to be with him. Together. One last time.

I took a minute to compose myself. The palms of my hands were supporting my weight as I sat on the smooth cement garden bench, leaning forward. As my fingers gripped the cool stone, I could see the sun cutting the tops of my bare feet in half. After taking a slow deep breath, I prayed. Not to a distant, angry, untouchable, unfeeling god, but to my good God, who happens to know a thing or two about father-son relationships. I don't think I uttered any words, but the thing about him is words aren't ever necessary. I simply acknowledged him and my need of him and opened my mind to receive the help he offered. He was there, with me, as he had been since I'd seen him in the baptistery and hung out in the closet as Alice.

We arrived in Orlando early Tuesday morning, having taken a red-eye flight, and drove straight to the hospital in time to see my dad and meet with my dear brother Charlie. No family should be without a Charlie! We packed up Dad's things and he was carefully loaded into the ambulance. I drove ahead to the house my parents had lived in since I was six. My sister Patti, who was staying there for a few short months pending a move to Raleigh, met me at the door. I set up camp in my small childhood bedroom. A translucent sticker still affixed to the window read, "We're glad you're here in Florida." I'd put it there after a trip to the beach when I was seven.

The front bedroom, where Patti was staying, had been my parents' master bedroom for twenty-five years. When my dad had both legs amputated, Mom and Dad renovated their home and added a large, handicap-accessible master suite. It had two twin-sized beds. Mom slept on her half of a Craftmatic adjustable bed, and only a few feet away was Dad's hospital bed equipped with every necessary gadget. Mom always made sure Dad received the very best care, first from her, then closely followed by his team of doctors, nurses, and home healthcare aids.

The paramedics carefully placed my dad in his bed

and the familiar sound of the compression mattress breathed in and out as it rotated the pressure under him. He was prone to blood clots and pressure sores. Oxygen was flowing through the cannulas into his nose, and the familiar comfort of his own home enveloped him. As the paramedics left, they bid my dad a fond farewell, having driven him to and from the hospital many times over the last two decades.

Family members arrived, filling in the house like a jigsaw puzzle. By the end of the second day, all of the pieces were in place. My oldest sister, Pam, was the final piece making it home, also having cut a trip short.

Neighbors, family, friends, and even some of Dad's former employees came and went through our house that Tuesday and Wednesday as if we were hosting a forty-eight-hour Christmas party. It was like a joyful reunion. The house was as a house should be, full of life, love, stories, and amazing food. Old friends and family who couldn't visit talked to my dad on the phone. He told stories that we were determined to remember. His primary doctors—the ones most of my family also saw—stopped by late in the evenings just to check on him and all of us—routine behavior for these dear men.

On Wednesday May 2, 2007, just after dinner, the hospice nurse told me it was okay to give him a shot of morphine. Being off dialysis, his body was unable to rid itself of impurities and became a cauldron of toxins. Between that and his broken bones, he was in unrelenting pain. I prepared the morphine and gave him the shot in the fatty part of his cheek inside his mouth. It was the quickest way to relieve his pain.

Later that night, I got ready for bed, and in the stillness of the house, my mind wouldn't release the sick feeling that Dad wouldn't wake up again. Before I could go to sleep in the twin bed underneath the window sticker telling me how good it was I was in Florida, I got up. I walked on the cold hardwood floor into my parents' dark room. The sound of Mom's CPAP breathing machine along with Dad's air mattress and oxygen created a symphonic melody. I couldn't remember a time in the last ten years when their room sounded different. With a hint of a nightlight coming from their bathroom and the red and green lights on various machines keeping my dad comfortable, the stage was set for the final scene of his life. I could barely see him as I leaned in close and touched his cool soft hand and said, "I love you, Dad." He was slightly startled, having already dozed off because of the morphine. He looked me in the eye, grabbed my arm across the cold rails of his hospital bed, and said in a very groggy voice, "I love you, Al."

I blinked the tears right out of my tired eyes and sent them cascading down my cheeks. I walked the length of the hallway, past my room, to the front bedroom where my sisters were quietly chatting. How providential. My sisters had been my dearest childhood friends. I might now be Alan Chambers, but a part of me will always be Cindy Brady. I begged my sisters to reassure me that Dad would have one more day awake. I needed to talk to him once more and to say things I'd not yet said. I longed to talk to him as a little boy does his daddy. I wanted more of him.

Pam tried to reassure me and Patti nodded in agreement, but I think we all knew he wouldn't wake up. I went to my room, closed the door, and sobbed. I called Leslie, who was staying at our home, just a few miles away, with our two toddlers. She did what she always does when I cry. She listened and said, "I'm sorry, honey." Nothing else needed to be said. In those words, I felt her strong grieving heart, her unfailing love for me, and her devotion to my dad.

I smelled the coffee well before 6:30 a.m. the next morning. Dad wasn't awake, but Mom was. She and I sat together on bar stools at the counter that had replaced the glass octagonal table in the remodel, and sipped the hot comforting brew.

"You alright?" I asked.

"Yeah. You?"

"Yeah," I answered. Both of our voices cracked as we answered each other and our eyes filled with tears.

The others slowly woke up and joined us. But Dad never did.

His hospice nurse summoned me around noon and pointed to the color of his fingernails and his style of breathing. It sounded as if he was excited and getting ready for a big race. Indeed, he was about to race from this life to the next.

With all of his kids, a few grandkids, and Leslie

gathered around his bed, I said, "Mom, he can hear you. Tell him everything you need to tell him. All of us should."

As each of us took turns telling him how much we loved him, how good he'd been to us, and that we would take care of Mom, tears were flowing freely. My mom leaned over Dad's left shoulder one last time and whispered to him in his left ear, saying things that I imagine only a lifelong companion can say. As she finished, my dad surrendered and joined God the Father. We watched his last breath and waited what seemed like minutes for the next. It didn't come and we knew he wasn't there any longer.

We had an hour or so before the funeral home came to get him. My mom sat with him for a while, and then I did. He wasn't there, but his body was. I touched his soft hands over and over again as if to etch them so deeply in my mind that I would never forget. All the years we'd prepared for him to go and I was not ready. I couldn't help but think back on our amazing journey. There had been a few years in childhood when I'd prayed he'd go, but those last thirteen years and eight months had been miraculously different, a pure gift.

"Daddy, I sit on your lap." Isaac's sweet toddler voice coming from the airplane seat next to me beckoned me back to the present. As he settled on my lap, laid his curly blond head on my chest, and covered up with his blanket, his eyes closed and mine drifted to the window. It was a clear June morning, indicated by the vastness of the sky above and the land below. The flight attendant asked me if I needed anything. I didn't. I had everything I needed. My vision narrowed to another memory of my dad.

Prior to 1993, our relationship was more like a rollercoaster. One moment he was at home dancing a little jig in his white V-neck T-shirt and light yellow Bermuda shorts. Seconds later he told me I looked like all the queers down at Lake Eola because I had turned up the collars on my layered pink and royal blue Lacoste shirts. He would bark at Fred and me for laughing at the dinner table, and afterward he would joyously give us hot Krispy Kreme donuts.

I didn't think there was anyone more different from me than my dad. And I was more than fine with that. As a kid, I didn't want to be like him. He was so much older and less physically fit than my friends' dads. He was fun and liked to shop and eat, but his moods could change on a dime. He was impatient and cussed like a sailor. He could peel the paint off of a barn with a tongue-lashing, and by sixth grade I felt like I was the barn with no paint left to be peeled. It was easier to steer clear of him than to ride the rollercoaster wondering whether I'd get crazy fun Dad or grouchy Dad.

But on July 3, 1993, the final day of my first Exodus International Conference, something happened that changed everything. Nearly one thousand men and women like me, fighting against their same-sex attraction, had shown up to participate in the weeklong conference. We worshiped, heard testimonies, and learned about how to live a life surrendered to Christ in the midst of our messy gay reality. It was, up to that point, the most amazing week of my life.

There among honest, desperate, humble believers who were offering what seemed impossible to give, I found the most honest Christians I'd ever met. Being able to freely admit our feelings, attractions, and relationships in a large Christian setting where just about everyone was like me was new and fresh. It wasn't the small office at Eleutheros with a handful of people. It wasn't The Parliament House with its lust-filled air. It wasn't even Discovery, where my story was known, but where I was a minority. This kind of freedom felt right and life giving. I had found gay life (at least the version of it at The Parliament House and in the jacuzzi) unsatisfactory and untrue to my innermost being; yet to revert to the closet of hiding myself like my childhood alter ego, Alice, meant certain death. I didn't want to live in either of those worlds. I was moving forward. More honesty. More disclosure. I believed God was in that kind of transparency, and I didn't care if it made anyone uncomfortable. God and I were good, and that is all that mattered.

During the last morning session of the conference, I was sitting in the balcony of Estes Chapel at Asbury Theological Seminary in Wilmore, Kentucky. It was strangely reminiscent of First Baptist Church of Winter Park, where I spent most of my childhood. I felt comfortable in Estes Chapel. I ventured up to the balcony for the first time. I was tired from an emotionally exhausting week — even for an extrovert. I was distracted. My ADHD was raging. The service seemed to be going long and I just wanted it to end so I could go about the business of socializing on my last day in ex-gay paradise. I hadn't sat through an entire service the whole week. I stayed for the best parts: worship; the testimony; Ross, the hilariously campy emcee; and portions of the speakers.

In the balcony, I could zone out without being noticed. Unsure what the keynote speaker was saying, my thoughts drifted to my dad, and I whined a little about him. At Exodus I heard that my unmet emotional needs from my dad contributed significantly to my homosexuality.

It is Dad's fault! He *made me gay,* I decided, as anger seethed from my pores. At age twenty-one, I was at least a decade into my bitterness against my dad. There were so many things on my list of what was wrong with him, and his unjust anger was at the top. Why was he so mad all the time?

I was sitting with my elbows on my knees and my hands holding up my head when I heard a familiar voice speak into my core. "Your pain doesn't matter more than your dad's pain. He's been hurt too. That's why he's treated you in the way he has. He's reacting to his own fear and pain."

That's not fair! I thought, but of course, my spirit was moved by this voice of truth and wisdom. I knew in that moment I needed to stop thinking of myself as a hurt child and my dad as a mean father. Instead, I needed to start thinking of him as my brother, who had endured far more pain than I ever could have borne or imagined. I knew, most important, that I needed to forgive him. The hardness of my heart shattered into a million tiny pieces.

This was one of many moments during my time at Exodus when God met me. Nowhere else did I experience anything similar. Not the Church. Not the bars. I'll always be thankful for Exodus and for the opportunity it gave me to seek my own path, to honestly seek God.

I got home the next day, my mom's sixty-second birthday, and told my parents that I needed to talk with them. I was ready to divulge my whole story and to offer my forgiveness. I did. I told them all about the conference and why I had attended.

"Dad, you were a very hard man to live with, and some of the ways you treated me made it very difficult to love you. But I have forgiven you and hope you will forgive me for holding onto bitterness and anger. I know your life hasn't been easy and that you were doing the best you could."

"I'm sorry too, Al," he said. He inched forward in the recliner he was sitting in and looked down as if to gather his thoughts.

What happened next, I never could have predicted. Slowly, as if he was carefully opening a bottle of shaken soda, he began to tell me his story. His voice was calm and his story clear, as if he'd been rehearsing it for years.

———— ∞ ————

I had already known that my dad was the product of an affair between the poor sixteen-year-old daughter of a Knoxville, Tennessee, ironworker and, from what we've pieced together, a wealthy college boy. The boy's family lived in the exclusive Sequoyah Hills neighborhood, far from the tracks they must have crossed to meet one another.

Such scandals were deeply shameful in the religious South in the late 1920s, so my pregnant grandmother traveled from her Knoxville home to Chattanooga to live in the Florence Crittenden Home for unwed mothers. She prepared to have her baby, which would promptly be placed for adoption. On January 21, 1928, my father was born and his mother decided to keep him—his father and paternal grandparents had up and moved to California. She brought him back to live on her parents' rented farm in a five-room house along with some of her other nine siblings.

By the time he was two, his grandmother placed him for adoption. Dad went to the Home for Friendless Babies, where Mrs. Hasley, the owner, a brutal woman who feared God and enforced his commandments, said things like, "Robert, if you touch the piano again, I'll take a hammer to your fingers." My dad was never able to get Mrs. Hasley's face or voice out of his head.

"She fed us kids one meal of ketchup sandwiches on thin white bread some days and nothing else on others.

I wore the same shoes for two years, which is why my arches are so high." As an adult, dad wore size eight shoes with custom-made insoles because he probably should have been a nine and a half.

"I was at the home for just a little while when Bess started working there." Dad remembered the day the teenage girl with the same color hair as his became his first and only friend. She was the less-well-to-do cousin of his suspected biological father and was on a mission. She took little Robert home with her nearly every weekend for a year. Bess Chambers lived with her parents, younger brother, and sister in a modest home in the middle-class neighborhood called Vestal just to the south of downtown Knoxville. The Chambers, a hardworking family with a stable income, fell in love with Robert, including Bess's father, Walter.

"Let me adopt this little boy or I am telling Bess to never bring him home again. My heart cannot bear his transience," he announced to his wife. At age three, Robert Palmer became Robert Lance Chambers.

Walter Chambers Sr. died of colon cancer six short years later, leaving my dad with a fifty-three-year-old mom forced to work multiple jobs and long hours. Bess was married and starting her own family by this time, and his other siblings were off doing their own thing.

By age twelve, Dad was making good money driving bootleg moonshine from Knoxville to Lexington on midnight runs. He and his buddies jumped off many a train truss onto watermelon trucks to steal late-night snacks.

He ran away from home often. He made it all the way down to New Orleans once and ended up in prison. He hadn't committed a crime. He was simply a homeless youth and a policeman believed homeless youths deserved to go to prison. A month into being incarcerated, he was regularly molested and beaten so badly by his adult cell-mate that one of the guards helped him escape one night, gave him some money, and told him to go home. Quickly. And never come back.

The abuse he suffered was so unbearable he wouldn't speak of it until that hot July afternoon in 1993 when he shared with my mom and me, for the first time ever, the horrific secrets of his childhood. We sat for hours and exchanged the life-giving gifts of unburdening secrets and shared forgiveness.

The nearly fourteen years that followed were very different for my dad and me. The redemption of our relationship was sort of a new birth. The new life, like blood being pumped from your heart to the tips of your toes, took a bit of time to work its way to all aspects of his personality and vocabulary, but it was flowing. He still had a propensity to occasionally bark and bite, but not a day went by that he didn't call me to tell me how much he loved me. He called all of my siblings daily, and he treated my mother as his most prized treasure. As hard and militaristic as he had been, he became that soft and tender. I didn't always know what to do with his sweetness. The transformation was amazing, though.

"Are you surprised that I am gay?" I asked one day.

"Or at least that those have been my feelings?" I don't know why I asked this question, but I think Dad's answer surprised me.

"I always suspected we would have a conversation like this. I am so proud of you for telling us. I am so proud of you for handling so much on your own. I haven't ever doubted your ability to do anything you set your mind to doing."

I learned to relate to my father in the absence of mistrust. He loved me and I loved him. That was that. I learned I was a lot more like him than I had believed. Our similarities were almost uncanny. His love was never something I questioned, but I *had* always wondered whether he liked me. I had long felt I was a bitter disappointment—the son who hated sports, lacked most stereotypical masculine traits, and seemed so different from him. But in those last years of his life, I knew I was dearly loved by my dad and deeply respected. I could see it when he looked at me.

There were times I wanted to blame being gay on my dad—on my upbringing—on the deficiencies in our relationship. But I cannot. It's not that easy. My attractions toward men were not his fault—they were not anyone's fault. They just are. Honestly, if fathering failures or shortcomings caused someone to be gay, there'd be a lot more gay people in the world. I cannot blame my father for doing the best he could. What I chose instead was to be in relationship with him. And he chose to be in relationship with me.

As the wheels of our airplane touched the runway in Los Angeles, I knew what I would say to the Exodus conference attendees. I would talk about the importance of forgiveness, and how I'd never truly known what it means to be a man until the day my dad bared his soul. My dad was vulnerable with me every day of those remaining thirteen years and eight months. He was my hero.

I entered the last half of my presidency at Exodus with Leslie, our two kids, Matt's statement about never being able to "be like me," and the legacy of my father heavy on my heart. I was determined to make sure that what I did in this life mattered. I was determined to peel back layers of pride, fear, and secrecy in the hope that I wouldn't make some of the same mistakes my father had.

CHAPTER 11

GOING OUT OF BUSINESS

"I'm going to resign from the hiring committee," I told Leslie over the phone. It was already May in 2001 and I had only a little over a month to prepare for my first in-person interview.

"I thought Bob wanted you on the committee," she said, "to represent the board and to help make sure that whoever they hire has a younger, more progressive voice."

A couple of weeks earlier, Bob Davies, then executive director of Exodus International, had officially announced his retirement. "Exodus needs to hire an executive director who is completely opposite of me," he'd said. His words to the board of directors, of which I had been a part for a year, were telling, and like E. F. Hutton, when the mild-mannered introvert spoke, people listened. "I never dreamed Exodus would grow to be what it is today. I don't have a vision for its future. We must hire someone who does. Someone who is gregarious, outgoing, connected, and full of vision. Someone a lot younger."

I told Leslie, "I've been thinking about it and I'm going

to resign from the committee so I can apply for the job myself." A silver-framed picture of Leslie and me from our wedding day sat on my desk and held my attention. I was content working at Calvary, where I was actually hired as an associate pastor in 1999, and I wasn't looking for a job, but the moment Bob told the Exodus board he was retiring, I had a hunch I would be his successor. There were others who seemed to be imminent heirs, but the sense that I needed to apply grew until it reached the point where I was ready to risk the comfortable, secure life Leslie and I were leading.

"I don't know. It's too much. It's too big a deal," she stated. She was probably the only other person on the planet who thought that if I applied, I'd actually get the job. And she knew I needed to be sure and to carefully count the costs, because there would be costs. It was a big deal.

A month later, at the Twenty-Sixth Annual Exodus Conference, I was in a basement appropriately named the Fireside Room interviewing for the job. Smoke from previously burned wood fires was thick on the walls and wreaking havoc on my sinuses. I sat across the table from the hiring committee. All six of them were people I'd known for years—friends and leaders within Exodus. They'd been surprised, shocked even, when I turned in my application. Up to that point, all they expected from me was a quick wit and an impetuous bent to push the boundaries of appropriate behavior. This was the final step in the interviewing process, and I was shocking them further. I had come prepared. I explained where I thought Exodus was and where we needed to go. I had a plan and used language they were familiar with.

"We're wandering around in the proverbial wilderness, and we don't know where we're going," I said. "We want to help people, but we're not unified in what we think is the best way to help, and there simply aren't enough of us. Based on the good I found at church, at Discovery and Calvary, I believe with all my heart that if Exodus can gain a positive posture within the Church, we will find the answers we are looking for. We, Exodus and all people with same sex attractions, will find our Promised Land in the Church. Our milk and honey is love, acceptance, reconciliation, and assimilation into the body of Christ—the Church. If we help the Church understand us, understand our lives, they'll be able to help others, even people we'll never have the opportunity to meet."

Alan Medinger, who had been the first executive director of Exodus, asked one final question. "Alan, what would success look like to you if we hired you as the executive director of Exodus?"

"Success, to me, looks like Exodus going out of business because the Church is doing its job," I said.

Someone lifted an audible amen. They all agreed, and a month later, they unanimously voted to hire me.

I loved working for Exodus. Eleutheros had provided a space for me as a confused teenager, and I wanted to grow that space for kids like me. Exodus was the umbrella under which local ministries could operate, and the umbrella needed to be strengthened if it was going to withstand the churning winds of the changing cultural climate. The evangelical church would be our sanctuary. There were states and countries without Exodus, but there were churches everywhere. I set out determined to make Exodus an organization the Christian church would embrace. We would have a unified vision of finding our place within the Church and a higher degree of professionalism with less of a mom and pop feel, and with increased exposure, we just might be able to help more people.

The challenges we faced had been in the making since Exodus's foundation and were decades old. We confronted the multiple subcultures (or mini kingdoms) built up within Exodus. These groups formed around ideological and theological differences. In an effort to "fix" humanity, some were losing sight of the reason we had come together in the first place.

———— ∞ ————

In 1976, I was a fairly happy child who occasionally pretended to be Alice, the USA celebrated its two-hundredth birthday, and Jimmy Carter and Gerald Ford contended for the White House. I didn't know anything about the issues fueling that election, but I remember my staunchly Republican parents voting for a Democrat for the first and last time in their lives and my mom stating that her recently deceased father, a lifelong Republican judge, was likely rolling over in his grave—an unnervingly clear picture for an imaginative four-year-old. While the bicentennial celebrations and election were big events in our household, something that later was far more personally significant was also developing.

A major battle was underway between the conservative Christian church and the growing gay rights movement. Each side took to its corner and position; the Church flaunting "homosexuality is an abomination" and the gays pushing their inalienable right to pursue happiness. In another corner of the ring, a new group was gathering that didn't fit into either of the other two. It wasn't considered newsworthy to most, but in October 1976, a handful of men and women met at Melodyland Christian Center, a charismatic megachurch in Anaheim, California, to fellowship, worship, pray, and strategize.

But this was no ordinary Christian conference. Of the sixty-three folks there, most were self-proclaimed ex-gays who came together to simply fellowship together. They shared a commonality in their beliefs about God and what the Bible said about sexuality, along with a growing frustration with their churches, which didn't seem to know what to do with them.

Ex-gay was a term first coined by Michael Bussee, then founder and leader of EXIT, the Ex-gay Intervention Team. EXIT was a ministry at Melodyland formed to help gay Christian men and women who wanted to "leave homosexuality" in pursuit of celibacy or heterosexuality. Michael along with a number of volunteers spearheaded the effort, which served as a catalyst for the gathering at his church. And while Michael has said on numerous occasions that these early ex-gay pioneers didn't necessarily think eradicating all same-sex attraction was possible, they were going to believe toward that end.

"Let's call it God Save the Queens," said one board member.

"How about Fruits of the Spirit or AC/DC: Transformers?" said another, laughing.

These initial board members had been chosen from a smattering of ex-gay ministries across the country. They deliberated for hours over a proper name and landed on Exodus. They believed that like the ancient Hebrews who were enslaved to and then delivered from their Egyptian oppressors, God would provide a way for this group of individuals to escape from what was understood to be the tyranny of homosexuality.

At the second conference in 1977, other nations were represented, such as Canada, England, and the Netherlands. The group became Exodus International. The conference became an annual event. There were thirty-eight conferences in all. I attended the last consecutive twenty-one of them, and Leslie the last sixteen.

From the firsthand accounts I have heard and the archives I've read, the first two years of Exodus were relatively peaceful, but like their exodic predecessors, the Israelites, it didn't take long for them to become dissatisfied and begin grumbling.

The year 1978 brought the first real dispute and schism. Should Exodus promote change—the ability of people to go from gay to straight—or should Exodus simply encourage celibacy? Is change, in the context of sexual attractions, possible? By the end of the 1978 conference, Exodus had split and a number of ministries and leaders who believed they should only encourage celibacy left the newly formed organization. For those who stayed, the idea of changing lined up with their theologies of pursuing personal righteousness. This would become the underlying goal of Exodus, and in hindsight, the beloved golden calf.

The year 1979 brought even more unrest as Michael Bussee and a leader in his ministry, Gary Cooper, announced they were leaving their wives and Exodus because they had fallen in love with one another. Michael and Gary had a commitment ceremony and stayed together until Gary passed away years later with Michael by his side.

Exodus continued to grow and "change is possible/ freedom from homosexuality is possible" became its binding mantra even when individuals and ministries disagreed on how to change or what to change. The idea of leaving homosexuality was attractive, and everyone was searching for the best route.

Groups looked for the answer in spiritual disciplines like prayer, Bible study, and confessing sins to accountability group members. One ministry in the 1980s was known for casting out demons, which is likely one of the reasons Exodus earned the reputation for being a "pray the gay away" organization. In these circles, man's sinful nature and the individual's responsibility to deny himself and take up his cross took center stage. If only you will do *these* things or go through *that* program or pray in *this* way, then God will meet you and your cravings will subside and you will be changed. Not everyone who followed the disciplines experienced a diminishing of homosexual attractions, and many left in shame, leaders included. They felt as if they had somehow let God down because their feelings didn't straighten out.

In the late '80s and throughout the '90s, the professional therapy movement came on the scene with all sorts of new scientific research, and Exodus linked arms with it. Dr. Joseph Nicolosi authored *Reparative Therapy for Male Homosexuality* and founded the National Association for the Research and Therapy of Homosexuality (NARTH). In layman's terms, reparative therapy is a niche psychotherapeutic model that suggests homosexuality is a developmental disorder caused by unmet relational needs beginning in the early developmental stages of a child's life and continuing through puberty. This hypothesis also reports a high percentage of homosexuals were victims of childhood sexual abuse. Because of these same-sex emotional and relational deficits, and sometimes sexual abuse, homosexuality, a reparative drive, like dissociative identity disorder (split personality), develops to meet the unmet needs. Reparative therapy isn't actually aimed at repairing; it just acknowledges the reparative aspect of the perceived disorder.

Reparative therapy, though never officially a programmatic element of Exodus, became the predominant way of thinking about the causes and treatment of homosexuality. Exodus was a Christian ministry at its core, unlike NARTH, but both professionals and lay leaders alike seemed to integrate the reparative model into the day-to-day of their work and ministry. The powerful merging of the spiritual and psychological seemed like a winning combination in the fight against any unwanted behavior.

"Is There a Gay-Gene?" made the cover of *Newsweek* in the early 1990s. Media reports more than suggested that science said yes, and society ran with it. For most within Exodus, the answer to the great gay-gene debate needed to be a resounding no. As Christians, we couldn't believe God would create us gay within the very fibers of our DNA and then tell us it was—we were—an abomination. There had to be another explanation of how it happened, so we could make it "un-happen." If it was a nurture issue, that would explain so much. It wasn't God's fault. It certainly wasn't our fault; we didn't choose to be gay. It was easy to be distracted by the slippery slope of the blame game. Let's blame it on our parents or culture or church.

Exodus saw an increase in professional counselors and licensed therapists who became a part of the network, and we enjoyed newfound legitimacy. Professionals backed up our biblical truth. While I am forever saying, "Everyone needs a good counselor," too many people who should have remained good listeners became quasi psychologists and offered their own *expert* advice.

Such was the atmosphere in the summer of 2001, when I applied for and was hired for the job of executive director, later retitled president, of Exodus International. We were Christians with same-sex attractions who believed that monogamous heterosexual marriage was the only God-ordained form of sexual expression. Few people in the organization believed we could simply "pray away the gay," and more and more we were acknowledging the multifaceted intricacies of what may "cause" an individual to have same-sex attractions. Most of us simply sought peace and reconciliation with God and our families. The culture was changing, we were changing, and we were trying to be more thoughtful as we plodded along our unmarked path.

———— ⬿⬿⬿ ————

From the day I was hired, I started making changes. A lot of them. Quickly. My way of doing things was loved by some and hated by others. After a short battle with one board member and with the support of the three remaining staff members, we moved the Exodus office from Seattle to Orlando. We studied board structures and changed ours to align with prominent ministries and successful businesses, adding members who weren't elected from within Exodus and who would bring in outside influence and experience. We strove to do everything with excellence and raised our support base by more than 200 percent, eventually raising enough for a down payment on a building.

In an effort to be a ministry that the Church would welcome into the fold, and to truly give this ministry back to the Church, we set up a network for churches willing to welcome and walk alongside people with same-sex attractions. We quickly had more churches than member ministries, and the size of our network more than doubled. People were getting it, even though a handful of member ministries felt threatened. They didn't think anyone outside Exodus could do the work we were trying to do, and they didn't want to lose their jobs.

We dabbled in the political arena, believing we could make a difference. Our beliefs aligned to the conservative right, but we were bothered by the ignorance in certain aspects of the established religious right. We shared our stories, hoping to influence people to think and speak more compassionately, but too often we were listened to only when it was convenient and when we could help promote an agenda. In 2007, I received three phone calls from three political and professional acquaintances. One from Mike Huckabee's campaign, one from Mitt Romney's campaign, and one from John McCain's campaign. I let them each know I wasn't ready to back a candidate, and I haven't heard from them since. I became disillusioned with the process, and on top of it all, we were alienating and marginalizing the very group of people we were trying to help.

We pulled out of all political groups after the passing of California's Proposition 8. I had spoken in favor of Prop 8 and against marriage equality, believing gay marriage threatened heterosexual marriage. The night Prop 8 passed in California, I watched the coverage on a Fox News split screen. On the right was a ballroom full of celebrating supporters, and on the left was a ballroom full of devastated opponents. Watching shattered families on the left trying to regroup after being told their relationships were less than and not equal to those on the right changed me. My marriage is strong, and I'll fight for it. I believe wholeheartedly in the institution, and I decided I would no longer fight against people who want the right to have what Leslie and I have.

After that, there were lots of ups and downs at Exodus. Tensions began to rise as our relevancy and unity began to crumble. Still, there's not been a single moment that Leslie or I regretted my applying for the job or getting the job or doing the job. There are those on the hiring committee who not only came to regret their decision to hire me but also became my fiercest critics. Such is life. It's likely that Exodus would still be in business if they'd hired someone else, but I am unalterably convinced God worked in the process and chose a foolish thing in this world (me) to confound the wise. After all, I believe closing Exodus was birthed in God's heart.

CHAPTER 12

THE 99.9 PERCENT

In March 2011, Leslie and I found ourselves tucked into a covert corner under a stairwell in a hotel lobby in Northern Ireland. It was the only private spot with a strong enough internet connection to watch a show we'd taped months earlier with Lisa Ling. It could have been cozy, but the floor-to-ceiling windows let in a frigid North Atlantic air along with the soft gray light. The Exodus office had been given a link to preview the show before it aired at home later that day. "It was okay. I think the damage can be controlled" was the discomforting report from one staff member who was able to watch it before we did. Shivering from both the cold and anxiety, Leslie and I watched, wondering what potentially irreparable damage I'd done.

I'd been wary of doing the show, *Our America with Lisa Ling*, on the brand-new Oprah Winfrey Network (OWN) but decided to go ahead with it when Lisa called personally and assured me of her good intentions. We began filming at the 2010 Exodus conference, and the show aired while we were in Northern Ireland. It revealed some weaknesses in Exodus, but that was to be expected. It seemed to be one of the first honest in-depth looks at Exodus and me. After watching, Leslie and I looked at each other with great relief and said, "Not bad." In fact, we thought it was really good.

We went upstairs, put the computer away, and enjoyed the rest of our trip in a part of the world that calls to our souls. We sat, bundled up, on the top open-air level of a tour bus in Belfast and were quieted by the region's murals. As we drove through the landscape of C. S. Lewis's childhood homeland, I'm fairly sure we saw a dryad in the lush forest on our right. We met—well, stood in line and shook hands with—the soon-to-be-married William and Kate. A news reporter, with her cameraman in tow, noticed my American accent and asked me what I thought about meeting the prince and soon-to-be duchess. She remarked that I was a natural on camera.

But at home, the damage my natural abilities had wrought would not be controlled.

The hour-long show had ended with Lisa and me sitting in a small chapel, our chairs facing each other, and with nothing between us. She sat at a comfortable angle, with her legs crossed and her hands folded, resting on her leg. My posture was similar. Her demeanor put me at ease. She asked, "Will there be gay people in heaven?"

I answered as I have every time I've been asked the question. "Do I think there are people [currently] living a gay life who are going to be in heaven? Of course I do. Is there condemnation for those who are in Christ? There is not. There are people who are living a gay Christian life. An active gay Christian life. God is the one who called them and has their heart. They are in relationship with God. Do I believe they will be in heaven? I do."

At the Exodus office, the phones rang relentlessly and in-boxes distended. Ministry partners and supporters challenged me on my closing statements and demanded I retract and apologize for them. I would not. I could not. If Exodus wasn't a safe haven for people in need of a judgment-free zone, then we were no different than the fundamentalist, legalistic, pharisaical parts of the Church we had once run from. "If actively gay people can't be Christians, then no one can," I retorted to my critics. I would not be controlled by threats of dissension and withheld financial support, and it was not my job to control anyone else's behavior.

The push and pull of this season was relentless. My critics on the right were pushing me to recant my "gays will be in heaven" comments, and my critics on the left, who I think saw the deepening cracks in the ex-gay narrative, were pulling at me for more disclosure. A month after the interview aired on *Our America*, I was back in Hollywood for another pivotal moment on camera.

"Alan, I was forbidden to play piano at Love in Action and was told it was a distraction and contributed to me being gay," KC said. I knew he was telling the truth. I'd heard accounts of equally ridiculous mandates from another young man who was told he couldn't wear Calvin Klein underwear because it would cause him to lust. KC and his husband, Larry Jansson, sat to my left, while Dr. Drew (Pinsky), host of the Headline News (HLN) show that bore his name, was to my right. Love in Action (LiA), a ministry that had long been looked upon as one of Exodus's most prestigious member ministries and the organization credited with being the first "ex-gay" ministry in the world, had an increasing number of former clients of their live-in program making ugly disclosures of their negative experiences at the ministry. I was Exodus's president and tightly tied to LiA's reputation, but not its daily operations. Still, I faced my accusers and yet also wanted to prove that my Exodus experience had been different from KC's and Larry's.

I swiveled in my chair to face KC. My once-folded hands were now extended toward these men as if to plead with my critics. "That's silly" was all that came out of my mouth, which was a silly response to KC's testimony of hurt. I desperately wanted to explain myself and to side with KC. I was always trying to explain myself. To defend Exodus. But as I started to honestly admit that I was at odds with Love in Action and many of their unorthodox practices, I was quickly put in my place and reminded I was complicit.

"Love in Action is one of the 250 organizations on *your* website. *You* promote it." Larry's comment was absolutely true. I might as well have been the one who told KC he shouldn't play the piano.

By their own admission, this couple's only consolation for living through the religious boot camp was meeting each other and falling in love. They'd faked their way through the program, graduated, and ended up marrying one another the next year.

I felt put in my place, and shamed. And an ongoing battle was raging within me. In moments like these, I wanted to close Exodus for good and fight for people like KC and Larry. And yet I loved Exodus and believed there was great potential for it to become more than it had been known for. I hoped we could remain an encouragement for the minority of people we had historically served and become advocates within the Church for LGBT people seeking inclusion and acceptance there. We were trying to make changes, but I understood that Exodus was light years from being what it needed to be. And what that was, I'm not sure I could have told you.

The Gay Christian Network (GCN) was founded in 2001 and is, according to their website, "a nonprofit Christian ministry dedicated to building bridges and offering support for those caught in the crossfire of one of today's most divisive culture wars."

Their membership "includes both those on side A (supporting same-sex marriage and relationships) and on side B (promoting celibacy for Christians with same-sex attractions)." To say many in their membership deeply disliked or at least deeply mistrusted Exodus and me is not an overstatement. I believed it was the perfect place to continue to try to make amends and show we were different, changing. I wanted to reconnect with lost friends, hopefully take down a few barriers, and make new friends.

In 2012, they hosted their annual conference in Orlando. I contacted Justin Lee, GCN's founder, and offered to sit in a room with him and the LGBT Christians attending the conference. Justin agreed and put together a panel of three former Exodus leaders and the two of us. Courageously, he offered it as a main evening session and was blasted by some LGBT bloggers, leaders, and supporters for allowing a man who represented deep heartache for so many to infiltrate such a space. It was an optional session, but the majority of the four hundred or more attendees packed the ballroom at the Hilton World Resort in Orlando. The moment I walked into the room, it was like someone flipped a switch and the electricity that flowed through the closed-circuit room could have powered Manhattan.

We noticed how eerily similar it looked to one of our events—like the alter ego episodes of *Seinfeld*. The nametag lanyards, their clothes, their hair, the small groups of guys walking in together, the small clusters of women already sitting down in the back of the room, and the few families—a mom and a dad and their young-adult child—scattered throughout the room made it feel like an Exodus conference. I knew some people by name. Most were cordial. Justin opened the service in prayer.

A worship band took the stage, and we sang songs that resonated in churches everywhere on any given Sunday morning. Turning our focus to God, we all relaxed a little.

Justin called the panel to the stage. Each of the other members spoke disparagingly of Exodus and challenged me as I listened. An hour and a half later, I took my ten-minute turn. I said a few things that were well received but considered heretical within other Christian circles—especially within Exodus. Justin wrapped the evening up and dismissed the crowd. Leslie and I stood just offstage and greeted people for hours. Folks waited in line to thank me for coming, a few needed to tell me how wrong I was and how much they had been hurt, and nearly every encounter ended with a hug. When we finally left the ballroom exhausted but grateful for the miracle that had just taken place, it was after 1:00 a.m.

The session aired on YouTube the next day. The negative response from Christians threatened to hijack everything I was trying to do at Exodus. I heard from people who were appalled that I addressed the crowd as my fellow brothers and sisters in Christ. "Honestly, it was a Christian conference; how else was I supposed to address them?" I responded over and over to hundreds of inquirers. I heard from people who were offended by the fact that I joked with the crowd about wishing I had a martini and a cigarette to help get me through the evening. Maybe I should have said I wished I had a bowl of ice cream, though ice cream was nowhere near strong enough. But most of all, I heard from folks who were frantic over my speaking a truth I had no idea was supposed to be a secret.

I said, "The majority of people whom I have met, and I would say the majority meaning 99.9 percent of them, have not experienced a change in their orientation or have gotten to a place where they can say that they could never be tempted or are not tempted in some way, or experience some level of same-sex attraction. The vast majority of people that I know do still experience some level of same-sex attraction."

People, especially a faction of Exodus leaders, hated this statement more than anything else I had ever said. Remember, Exodus was all about change from gay to ex-gay, and the leadership at Exodus took this as an admission that we were failures and hiding something. It was no such thing. I simply admitted we were human. Maybe I could have phrased it better, I don't know. But I said it. And to this day, I stand by the message.

In the years that have followed, even though oh-so-many people would love to discredit me, not one person has come forward to disagree with me. Not one has said my statement was untrue. When I used the 99.9 percent statistic, I had one female friend in mind as the 0.1 percent. At the time she was the only person who had said she had no residual same-sex attractions, but she has now written a book and, though very happily married to a man, stated she easily could have ended up content in life with a woman.

Our reputation was becoming increasingly negative on many fronts. Depending on who was talking, we were either too political or not political enough. Too conservative or too liberal. While one group criticized us for not promoting heterosexuality, a prominent church left our membership because I was married to Leslie. We were too reliant on prayer and concurrently too reliant on professional counseling. The stories that might have been told about how people were helped through Exodus were overshadowed by the stories of those who were hurt.

The infrastructure of Exodus had weakened, so with the backing of the staff and board, one of the most respected Exodus pioneers and I came up with what we believed were four possible options for the future of Exodus. We shared them with our leaders. We could:

- *Stay the same.* This was not a real option. I stated I wouldn't continue as president if this were the consensus.

- *Rebrand.* I felt like this was similar to Kentucky Fried Chicken changing its name to KFC simply to sell more fried chicken. I had lost faith in too much of what we were trying to sell, and so this too was not a real option.

- *Modify.* On the morning I was to present this alternative, while it was still dark outside, Leslie and I sat in bed and looked up the meaning of the word. It didn't seem like it carried enough weight for the amount of change necessary until we discovered that mutate is a synonym. Mutate means to change your DNA, the very fabric of your being. God's grace could change our very makeup. To modify, to mutate, became the option I hoped Exodus would embrace.

- *Shut down.* I was already privately talking with friends about shutting Exodus down when I presented this possibility to the leaders. Some saw the problems as I did and understood, but many said they didn't want to shut down because they liked each other and being a part of a network. Their willingness to trump the needs of those they were serving in order to meet their own desire for community made me question whether modifying would be enough.

During this week, a small group of disgruntled leaders rallied as they took advantage of face-to-face interactions, and a clear leader emerged. He, along with others, began making plans for a new Exodus. Not long after the conference, this group publicly called for my resignation. They believed my promotion of the Church as the place where people should go for support was the downfall of Exodus. They believed the only way for Exodus to survive was to get rid of the churches and emphasize the ministries again. A woman from this group passionately mocked me and my idea of helping parents to love and accept their gay children. At the leadership conference, she verbally vomited, "When a parent with a gay child comes to our ministry, it is our duty to warn them that their child is in danger of going to hell." Some in this group were just tired and wanted Exodus to be like it was back in the good ole days.

By the autumn of 2012, the sifting was almost complete. At our Made for More conference, I announced that Exodus would no longer support or recommend reparative therapy. Many within the conservative Christian crowd stopped supporting Exodus when I pulled this trigger. I was called a heretic and so many other things. Christian periodicals and talk shows blasted me. Theologians debunked me and friends unfriended me, literally, on Facebook. Staff members quit and two board members resigned. And nearly everyone who left Exodus gravitated toward a new organization, called The Restored Hope Network, filled with many of the original Exodus ministries and leaders and their hardline funda-mentalist ideas.

Those who stayed, even if they didn't agree with everything we were doing, were willing to walk through the minefields with us. They wanted to promote the best that Exodus had to offer. They wanted to walk hand in hand with people who were hurting. They wanted to help. They wanted, most of all, to promote God's love. We began to experience levels of excitement, growth, and unity we had not known previously. We were hurting financially, but money wasn't ever our main concern.

This season at Exodus was among my favorite as its president. We weren't fighting. No one was complaining. The leaders who had once been the most critical of their peers were gone and had started a new ministry—ironically with each other. It was peaceful, and we did some really great work. But it wasn't to last long.

————— ◦◦◦ —————

With internal resistance to my leadership and to increasing transparency waning, the opposition from those outside of Exodus became palpable, and my next step became clear.

In February 2013, I texted Lisa Ling and asked her if she would consider doing another show with me. It was time to apologize publicly to those who had been hurt by Exodus. I had been privately apologizing for the "bad" I had heard about in the stories of people who had hated Exodus for years; it was time to do so publicly. I told Lisa I had been interacting with people who had been hurt by Exodus—guys like KC and Larry—and was reevaluating some of my actions and words. I wanted to apologize for things I had done too. She immediately said yes.

She asked if I would agree to give the apology to a live group of people called "ex-gay survivors." Some of these people had been connected to an Exodus ministry; some of them had been leaders within those ministries. Some of them hadn't been associated with Exodus at all. Michael Bussee, one of the founders of Exodus, would pull the group together. I would have no control over who was in the group. I agreed. Addressing people in person, seeing their faces and allowing them to see mine, was the only way to properly apologize. I would contrive none of it.

In April 2013, the cameras were rolling as Leslie and I walked into the basement of the fellowship hall of West Hollywood Presbyterian Church in California. Spotlights shone on thirteen people sitting in chairs arranged like a horseshoe. Two empty seats awaited us at one of the open ends. I sat on the very end, Leslie to my right, and two good friends next to her. Of the fifteen of us sitting under the lights, eight were complete strangers to me. Somewhere in the dark corners, another dear friend who accompanied us stood among a dozen or so others looking on.

Lisa began. Then Michael Bussee took charge as the leader of this quasi support group. And one by one, each of the others told us just what they thought. I remember all of their issues with Exodus and the Church in near detail, and I feel their pain as if it were yesterday. I remember Jerry, whose ex-wife and pastor didn't allow him to attend his son's funeral because he was gay. I remember Gail's tight curls framing her face as she passionately read her poem that likened me to Hitler. I remember Art standing up and walking toward me to drop a pile of his medical bills on my lap. Sean, the young war veteran, talked about going into a closet, taking out a gun, and putting it in his mouth. Brad, our friend and my former employee, had been denied the Eucharist in his church because he was gay. Chris, a pastor, had divorced his wife and was devastated over his broken family. Lisa had tears running down her cheeks, spilling onto her light blue denim shirt. Julie told a different story. She was gay and celibate and a friend of Exodus.

Then Leslie spoke, and the cameramen and producers later said it changed the atmosphere in the room. She made us flesh-and-blood humans by being herself. It was obvious that she wasn't some naive or ignorant wife, that she was a thoughtful, smart, and trustworthy woman. When Jerry acknowledged that we might actually be good people, Leslie responded, "Thank you for recognizing Alan isn't a monster but a person. That we have feelings too."

And then I apologized. I read my apology because I didn't want to mess it up. It was insufficient, and I would add more at a later date, but that day it was all I had. It was without agenda or condition—a beginning.

During the show, Jerry also asked a tough question. "Based on all of the changes at Exodus, what does Exodus actually exist for now?" I answered halfheartedly about our diminished services, and he abrasively pressed for more clarity.

My mind raced as I searched for an answer that would appease him and me. I didn't have one. It was the most awkward moment on the show. I can handle being yelled at, hearing horror stories, and saying I'm sorry. But not having an answer to the fundamental question, What do you believe? shook my core. I think I answered Jerry by saying, "We'll have to see." It's the same vague answer I often give my kids when I know full well we aren't going to do anything.

The cameras continued to roll as we stood up and began milling around the room. It had been an exhausting day. We smiled at one another and hugged one another. The tension, if not gone, was at least eased. It was overwhelming and restorative. It had been awful and somehow wonderful, and it all happened in a church basement and would be shared with a cloud of witnesses just six weeks later on national television.

One of the guys in the group was silent throughout the entire three hour and twenty-five minute taping. Christian had been a part of each of Lisa Ling's "Pray the Gay Away?" episodes of *Our America* over the course of the last three years. He appeared in the first show as the protege of an ex-gay leader in Minneapolis who was in the process of saving him from himself. I had been overwhelmed by his story and moved with great compassion. He was an artist, and the first episode had highlighted his work. Just over a year later, in the second episode, Christian was presented as someone who had cleaned up, was "less gay," and according to his ex-gay mentor was becoming interested in girls. When Lisa and Christian walked into his apartment this time, his extensive artwork was gone. His apartment wiped clean of all the fun abstract creations that had once filled it. It was neat, tidy, and awful, suggesting that maybe it was his art, like KC's piano playing, that made him gay.

Just before the basement show—the third episode—Christian and I had connected online for the first time. He had previously avoided me because his mentor found me dangerous. It was clear he was no longer connected with her and therefore was more interested and able to talk with me. His art was back and his ability to enjoy life seemed to be returning. The episode's final shot was Christian and me hugging and posing for a photo cheek to cheek.

While the shot of Christian and me was memorable, the words of Michael Bussee in the middle of the show rang loudest.

"Shut it down. Shut Exodus down. Don't change it. Don't do anything. Just shut it down." Little did he know that I was already thinking toward that end. It was a powerful moment, with both founder and finisher in the room together.

Leslie and I returned home completely changed. Within a few weeks' time, while the show and Exodus's future were constantly on my mind, our director of business affairs came into my office.

"I'm sorry to bother you. I know you have a lot on your mind," she said, taking a seat.

I was sitting at my desk and had been thinking about the basement and the ministries who were still with us. I was thinking about the staff I adored and about my kids. I was thinking about the church bulletin Leslie had just shown me from March 2012 with a note she'd scribbled on it saying, "We might just lose everything because of this grace stuff." I was thinking about the conference schedule we were going to have to drastically alter because of the unprecedented and shockingly low number of registrants.

The conference was only a few weeks away, and we were pressed to finalize the schedule. I was thinking about its theme, "True Story," and how the stories of the men and women I'd just encountered changed me forever. I was thinking about my true story and the positive role Exodus played in it. I was thinking about the men and women and the parents and the couples and the youth involved at Exodus, those who would be at the conference and who looked to us for help. I looked at Janine, my coworker and friend since high school.

"No worries. Have a seat." *Strange,* I thought, *that's just where Matt sat when he said he'd never be like me.* She was just as uneasy as he had been. She held financial documents and a pad of paper with endless notes in one hand and a purple gel pen in the other.

"I just got off the phone with our accountants, and they're worried," she began, looking at her notes. "The conference numbers and donations are so low, they don't think we'll make it through the summer. I've been offered another job, and I'm going to take it. I start there in two weeks. I can train someone else to do my job, and I don't know that there is anything for us to do except to let the rest of the staff know."

I gathered the staff that afternoon and together, as dear friends, we decided how to proceed. Leslie's salary would be cut immediately, and she would work through the conference as a volunteer. Randy proposed he take a drastic pay cut. David would take another job post-conference. Chris and Leah would be laid off. Stephanie would stay at home with her growing family. Scott would stay on and become a true Scott-of-all-trades.

Days later as I drove down my beloved Park Avenue on Wednesday morning, May 29, having just had my weekly breakfast with some of my best pals, I felt I heard God speak clearly, and in that moment, I knew what the next step would have to be.

CHAPTER 13

GRACE

On Father's Day, June 16, 2013, in the wee hours of the morning, I snuggled with my kids and kissed them good-bye. Even though it was 4:00 a.m., my sweet Molly Grace drew me a picture to take with me on my trip. It was of the two of us standing hand in hand. Then Leslie and I and our newly shrunken staff set off for what would be the last Exodus conference—ever. We had just over 250 people registered—a far cry from the crowds of previous years. Leslie loved the conference like a third child and tried to bolster my enthusiasm for the event, but I was exhausted. What was once exciting was now a chore. But it had to be business as usual. Leslie and the team would devote Monday to sorting out two pallets' worth of conference paraphernalia: name badges, signage, T-shirts, conference workbooks, and room assignments. The board would be meeting on Tuesday, with closing Exodus as our primary agenda item. Closing seemed to be inevitable, but none of us knew exactly how it would happen. I was scheduled to open the conference on Wednesday night and had no idea what I was going to say. A part of me felt it was going to be like *Weekend at Bernie's* and we were just propping up a corpse, but I knew there was a real life-giving message to share. Thursday night the third Lisa Ling "Pray the Gay Away?" episode would air and the world would be privy to all that happened in that church basement in West Hollywood.

We arrived at the conference center just after lunch and checked into our room, which would be home for the next tumultuous week. The room was sparse with two twin beds hugging parallel walls. It had a large window that let in a lifeline of sunshine and fresh air while simultaneously allowing people walking by on the sidewalk below to peer in. Later in the week, my heart and soul would be just as open and vulnerable. I unpacked my suitcases and rearranged the room, pushing the two beds together and ordering the haphazardly placed utilitarian dressers and desks. My mind was also unpacking—short and poignant vignettes from the past—as I contemplated the near future.

"Our witness must be like a velvet brick," explained a pastor friend from a local church. He was addressing a chapel full of Exodus leaders at our 2007 leadership conference. "The truth is the brick. It's hard and unchanging. The velvet surrounding the brick is grace. We must, as believers, be soft to the touch. Unabrasive. When our velvet begins to wear thin, we must ask the Lord to repair it."

I thought that meant that it was up to us to share the block-hard truth of Jesus, as long as we shared it nicely. Nicely was supposed to be the grace. The truth, I believed him to say, was thick and weighty. God's Word, his law, and his ways are hard in this life. Grace seemed to be soft, and its main function to balance the truth. God, I concluded from this man, is 100 percent grace and 100 percent truth—a walking contradiction. We might indeed be saved by grace, but at the time, I believed the truth was that we are perfected by what we do or don't do daily on planet earth.

Six years later, I sat on my makeshift double bed looking out the window at nothing in particular and realized I had laid down the idea of the velvet brick long ago. I could no longer condemn anyone, me included, based on behavior, because God doesn't. There's no life in condemnation or constantly focusing on what's right and what's wrong, what's good and what's bad. After all, it was humanity's hunger to define good and evil that got poor Adam and Eve in trouble all those years ago. Good and evil is a distraction, a detour. There's no life there. God's grace destroyed everything that could separate us from his love. God's love is the truth. God's love brings life. Grace doesn't balance truth or soften it. It just is the truth.

I could no longer mix the life-giving good news—that in Jesus, nothing can separate us from God—with the deadly message that our good behavior or *self*-righteousness affects our standing with God. Velvet or not, that brick wounds and kills.

Grace and love would be the truth guiding the board and me as we voted to close Exodus. Grace would guide me as I publicly released my apology—an extended version—to the gay community via the newswire hours before my opening (and closing) address. Grace led me as I prepared that final address to the conference attendees. It held me together as I did the hardest thing I'd ever done. Grace had changed everything for me, and it was about to take center stage, in its purest form, at Exodus without compromise. This would be my exodus.

⎯⎯⎯⎯⎯⎯⎯ ⊱⊰ ⎯⎯⎯⎯⎯⎯⎯

"For the last eighteen months, Exodus has been embroiled in a scandal," I said to the crowd three days later on opening night. The room was so still and quiet. Had someone actually had a pin handy and dropped it, I'd have heard it. We all could have. It was the eye of the storm, a hush between violent bands of torrential verbal and emotional rains. The right side of the hurricane had passed and cracked the shoddy foundations once laid at Exodus. In the eye, people were either looking for other shelters that promised to hold up under drastic conditions, or they rested, trusting what they knew would remain after the storm passed. The left side of the storm could be equally devastating. The storm, in its entirety, would clear away overgrowth and debris and hopefully allow for new growth.

I continued, "It is a scandal over who can go to heaven and whether we should be honest about the presence of temptation. I'm not smart enough to orchestrate such a scandal, and therefore I am convinced that the scandal is of God's making." Multitudes joined us via LiveStream, giving my last keynote address the largest audience in Exodus's history. I stood onstage knowing I needed to speak clearly to every faction, every critic, every friend. Only one message was burning deep within, and only one was worth risking everything in the next wave of storms that would surely come. God the Father, in perfect concert with Jesus and the Holy Spirit, is full of one truth: that he is fully grace. Pure grace.

"We in the Church have been motivated by fear. It is our fear that keeps us straight. It is our fear that causes us to look a certain way and act a certain way. It is our fear that has caused us to treat anyone who doesn't also act in a certain way like sinners in the hands of an angry God.

"Exodus International has become something that it wasn't intended to be. I believe the major failure of Exodus is that it promised to be completely different from the religious system that forced its creation and yet became a religious institution of rules and regulations focused on behavior management and short on grace. It's time our message changes to be one of hope and love and grace. It is for these reasons and other reasons that we, the board of directors of Exodus International and many within our leadership, believe it's time for Exodus to close."

Less than a month before the conference, and less than a month after the epic basement encounter with ex-gay survivors, I'd had a "God speaks" moment. I was driving down my favorite street after having breakfast with a group of guy friends I meet with each Wednesday. In my mind, I saw a picture of someone on life support. I immediately knew the person was dead and someone needed to pull the plug and let that person be at peace. I simultaneously knew it wasn't a person. It was Exodus. And God was saying to me, "Time to pull the plug on your dear friend and let him die with dignity." I drove to the Exodus building, walked into my office, closed the door, and wrote an email to my board.

In the email I shared about a dear friend of ours who'd lost her battle with cancer, how before she died she had asked her husband to take her off of his heart so he could love another. I told the board, "I sensed I was supposed to take Exodus off my heart so I could love another." At that point I thought "another" was another organization. Today, as I write this chapter, I believe "another" is people. All people. Certainly the LGBT community. Leslie and I have found great joy just being able to accept people for who they are—our kids, our families, our neighbors, and strangers.

I continued, "Today I truly believe I heard God say that Exodus is on life support and it is time to pull the plug. My desire is to see this move fairly quickly. I would even like to announce something at the conference, which means we need to tell our friends in the association. I realize this is fast, but many of us have been thinking about it for some time and there will never be an easier time to say goodbye."

I shared this letter with our entire membership days after I wrote it. The majority of leaders who responded were sad, but not surprised. At the conference, our board unanimously agreed to close Exodus International. And on June 19, 2013, I announced on opening night of the Thirty-Eighth Annual Exodus Freedom Conference that Exodus would close for good. It was the only time in my history as president, having opened twelve conferences, that the room was still and quiet when I finished. No applause. No one moved. There were a few sniffles, but it was eerily still like a village that had just been bombed and was still too shell-shocked to move or to look to others for consolation.

I stepped off the stage and walked down the aisle through the crowd to the back door. I didn't look at anyone. Holland Davis, my faithful friend and worship leader at Exodus since 2000, walked onstage and pastored the crowd. I was late for an interview with Jeff Chu, who was doing a story for *The Atlantic* that would be online by morning. It was the first interview I did as the former president of Exodus International.

The conference would continue for the next several days, and our staff did all they could to offer everything we knew about life for those attending. But I wasn't around much, because the news about Exodus had spread like wildfire after my speech, and the next two days I spent from sunup to sundown talking to reporters, everyone from the most rural newspaper in Pennsylvania to Anderson Cooper on CNN.

———— ∞∞ ————

"Alan," she said. She was in her midforties and wore a silver bob. "I am leaving before the last session tonight to go home to my son and daughter, but I need to thank you from the bottom of my heart. My daughter is a lesbian, and we have a good relationship. My son is transgender and hasn't spoken to me in months—until today." This sweet mom began to cry and grabbed my hand. "My son is now Tiffany, and she called me just a few minutes ago and told me she watched your opening-night speech with her sister. Both of my children said they weren't sure there even was a God until Wednesday night when they saw God in you. I'm going home today to my kids to love them as they are and to go to church with them tomorrow for the first time in a long time. Thank you for helping to restore my family. You did the right thing."

Words cannot describe how much that meant to me.

There were a lot of reasons we closed Exodus. But the single greatest reason was because of grace. In a world where people are clamoring for position and demanding clear declarations for or against all things gay, Leslie and I choose grace. We love God and we love people. We are joyfully immersed in life on planet earth with all its glory, destruction, and complexity, with people who are beautiful and messy.

CHAPTER 14

WHITE COUCHES

"How much are you selling your house for?" During our two-day estate sale in October 2014, we were asked this question dozens of times. Women and men alike, young and old, with families and without, single and married, gave us their business cards or scribbled their numbers on scraps of paper. I got an email from a lady through our blog and a handwritten letter from a lesbian couple, all asking us to sell them our beloved home.

We don't live in the Taj Mahal. Our house is a typical 1966 ranch-style home with four bedrooms, two baths, a two-car garage, and what we've affectionately called a one-butt kitchen. There's a wall in the garage with the annual measurements of our kids' changing heights, a small brown scrape on the family room ceiling where the 2011 Christmas tree hit after I'd impatiently yanked it out of the stand during cleanup, and a slight chip in the stucco just as you enter the garage from the driveway where my father-in-law accidentally clipped the house with our car on Thanksgiving in 2008.

Our neighborhood isn't gated. Our street is off the beaten path. If you drive down our lane, which is lined with massive oaks that provide a shady canopy to each of the ten houses, my neighbors and I will stare, knowing instantly whether you are visiting or lost. We will warn you with expressions that say, "We know everything that happens here." It's true, we do.

Although normal by most standards, our house does possess a special charm that most people who enter seem to notice. Leslie and I, and our kids for that matter, have given ourselves to every square inch of it. We love design and have taken enormous amounts of pride in the work we've put into making our home beautiful and inviting. We have painted the inside so many times because we can't just test a swatch of color; we have to see the whole room in it. On more than one occasion, we've painted a room, hated the color, and started over again in the wee hours of the morning—like the summer we closed Exodus, while Leslie's dad was in the hospital, when we painted our bedroom purple. Big mistake. We're collectors of beautiful treasures and family heirlooms, and the neighbor's family heirlooms, and strangers' family heirlooms acquired at our favorite weekly estate sales, and so on. We can place things and create warm and inviting spaces like nobody's business.

Our house has been our refuge. We hoped never to leave it.

By the end of 2011, before we closed Exodus, our novice understanding of God's unfathomable grace began to grow clearer and clearer, and we continued to see enormous cracks in the foundation that Exodus had set in us. We saw the danger of calling people "good" or "whole" or "healthy" or "healed" in relation to their sexual narrative. We have come to believe that in Christ, no amount of good or bad deeds can make us more or less righteous. The truth became simple: God is grace.

The grace revelation began to overflow in Leslie and me to the point where we could no longer keep the lid on our passion for it. We felt an almost life-or-death need to share it with the masses, as well as the garbage man, the cashier at the supermarket, and the bank teller. My interviews on television, radio, and print became, I believe, a lot more thoughtful, outwardly contemplative, and honest. My speaking engagements followed suit. I'd always affirmed someone's right to live the life they wanted and never disputed someone's salvation. I'd always told parents to love their kids and pursue relationship with them (and their partners) no matter what. But I found myself moving further toward a position I found politically and spiritually liberal because there was no other way to apply grace.

Soon, because of our outspoken view on grace and the murmurs from a few within the Exodus membership, and because some donors decided not to give, claiming I was sliding down a slippery liberal and heretical slope (wheeeee!), Leslie and I remarked to each other, "We might lose everything because of grace."

In August 2011, Leslie's folks sold their home in Fresno and relocated cross-country to Winter Park to build a house nearby. While they were waiting for their home to be built, they lived with us for ten months, and it was a very lovely time for us all. "Good thing you're building a big house with an upstairs," Leslie said with a laugh one day. "We might be living with you soon."

"Come on! At least we know we can do it," her mom responded, in close quarters with Leslie in our one-butt kitchen.

It was said in jest, but deep down, Leslie and I both knew that our new stance on grace could cost us our jobs. Like the woman at the well who couldn't shut up about Jesus after he offered her living water, Leslie and I couldn't, wouldn't, shut up about the good news of grace.

———— ∞∞∞ ————

In August 2014, about a year after we closed Exodus, Leslie and I were nestled into our favorite corners on our his-and-hers goose-down-feather-filled white couches. Though it was summer—with the temperature already approaching eighty, the humidity climbing steadily toward 100 percent, and the air-conditioning blowing— we had one of our sunroom windows open, through which we could hear the peaceful patter of our fountain cascading one tier to another on the far side of our pool.

It was 6:00 a.m., and Leslie was on her second cup of coffee. I laid down my latest issue of *Southern Living* and said, "I think we should sell the house, put things we love in storage, have an estate sale for the rest, and move in with your mom." I had done what I always did when I got one of my life-altering thoughts; I shared it quickly (so as not to allow the ADHD "look it's a bird" syndrome to steal this one away). Leslie has become quite accustomed to these paroxysms, and it's one of the quadrillion things that reinforce my unwavering belief that she and I were meant for each other. She never gets knocked over by my force, and in fact, we are a great team.

We moved out of our house on October 17, 2014, just after our estate sale. We chose to rent our home because we felt uncertain about closing that chapter irrevocably. Leaving neighbors we loved like family, a house where every milestone in our children's lives had been reached, and rooms we'd touched every last inch of with care, we sorted everything we owned into four groups: take, store, sell, or donate. Only necessary items could be taken. We rented a large storage unit for family heirlooms and treasured pieces of furniture we hoped to enjoy again back in our beloved house or in another we might come to love as much, took some treasures with us, gave some treasures to family and friends we could neither keep nor bring ourselves to sell, and purged everything else. During the process, an astonishing number of friends asked the same question: "Are you by any chance selling the white couches?"

To each and every one of them we responded with a firm, "Nope."

The slipcovered white couches that I purchased at

an estate sale a couple of years earlier for a quarter of their value are among the treasured items we reluctantly needed to store.

During the sixteen months between leaving Exodus and moving out of our home, our favorite white couches became home base and a much needed place of refuge. Those white couches served as a cocoon for Leslie, Isaac, Molly, and me. They're where Leslie and I started our day, every morning, drinking our first cup of coffee. They're where we occasionally napped on Sunday afternoon or just closed our eyes to rest. They are where we made funeral plans for Leslie's dad, who died of heart failure in August 2013. On those precious white couches our kids had sleepovers, as did some of the Exodus youth who spent a long weekend with us six months after closing Exodus. We drafted the proposal for this book on the white couches with the aid of dear friends Dr. Kathy Koch, Randy Thomas, and DJ Snell, and Leslie and I wrote the first draft of our book on the white couches. I spoke with countless people from those white couches in person, via email, and on the phone: new friends, old friends, and friends choosing to resign their friendship. I spoke with media personalities like Lisa Ling and Anderson Cooper from my favorite spot on one of the white couches and worked on the seemingly endless task of closing a nearly forty-year-old ministry.

Those white couches saw us through the mind-numbingly turbulent first few months post-Exodus, through the waves of feeling defensive and nearly bitter, and ultimately to the absolutely peace-filled final months in our sanctuary of a home. On the white couches, we experienced and decided to devote ourselves to only those things that bring life, the goodness of the Lord in the land of the living. And together, to loving and serving others.

In the comfort and solace of the white couches, I made new friends over the phone with people like Brian McLaren, who allowed me to call him and process my new life on the other side of the line in the sand. On the phone, seated on those white couches, I listened to dozens of nineteen- to twenty-year-olds tell me their stories of being gay and Christian and asking me how to proceed. They asked me about how to move forward in dating girls, how to break up with girls, whether marriage was something they should consider, and how to tell their loved ones they were embracing their gay life.

From those white couches I also heard from conservative pastor friends who hadn't been sure about my sanity or decision to close Exodus, but now called because their children were coming out and they needed to talk to a friend who understood.

Storing our white couches and renting our charming fortress to strangers was hard. Months into living at my mother-in-law's beautiful house, but in spaces much smaller than we are accustomed, it is still hard. But it is necessary. It is healing us.

Closing Exodus International for the reasons we did not only ruined our reputation in many circles, it also drastically altered our financial portfolio. Leslie's scribbled note to me on her Sunday church bulletin stating we might just lose everything because of grace wasn't so far off. Many claim we were making millions at Exodus off of innocent victims. Arguing the truth that such a thing is utterly ridiculous won't change their minds, but we can agree on this: Exodus needed to close and that's coming from me, one of the movement's greatest success stories.

And post-Exodus I have spent countless hours on those couches sorting out the truth of my story and editing out the embellishments that stemmed from years of finessing a message that made my reality seem more spiritually superior than that of my gay-identified counterparts.

I spent sixteen months on those white couches going over and over my successes and failures, trying to heal from decades of criticism, fear, and anxiety and trying to figure out what someone like me does now. The words of one critic often ring in my head: "Alan has no marketable skills. What will he do now?"

We don't have our white couches as we finish this book. We are displaced and trying to figure out what we will do professionally in the future. Our white couches are safely tucked in storage. They are awaiting a reunion, one in which Leslie will sit across from me and we will toast a hard day's work, having moved them back into the same spot from which they came, or a new spot in a yet-to-be determined location. On that day we will be older, wiser, and breathing more easily than in the season that led us to pack them away.

STAY IN TOUCH WITH THE CHAMBERS

To Book Alan and/or Leslie for an Event
Info@Legacy-Management.com
Legacy, LLC 407-705-3460

On the Web
www.AlanChambers.org

On Social Media
Twitter
@LeslieMChambers
@AlanMChambers
@MyExodusBook

Facebook
www.Facebook.com/AlanManningChambers

Instagram
www.Instagram.com/AlanMChambers

Pinterest
www.Pinterest.com/ChambersAlanM